Policing in Wartime: One Mountie's Story

WILLIAM KELLY

WITH

NORA HICKSON KELLY

Centax Books
Publishing Solutions/PW Group
Regina, Saskatchewan, Canada

Policing in Wartime: One Mountie's Story
by
William Kelly with Nora Hickson Kelly

First Printing – July 1999

**Co-published by RCMP Millenium Foundation
and by Publishing Solutions, PW Group**

Canadian Cataloguing in Publication Data

Kelly, William

Policing in wartime

Co-published by RCMP Millenium Projects.
ISBN 1-894022-31-9

1. Kelly, William, 1911-   2. Royal Canadian Mounted
Police--Biography.   3. Police--Canada--Biography.
4. Canada--History--1939-1945.   I. Keily, Nora (Nora
Hickson).   II. RCMP Millenium Projects.   III. Title.

FC3216.3.K45A3 1999a   363.2'0971'09044   C99-920103-4
HV8158.7.R69K443 1999

Cover and page design by Brian Danchuk, Brian Danchuk Design
Page typesetting and formatting by Holly Sentz

**Designed, Printed, and Published in Canada by:
Centax Books/Publishing Solutions/PW Group**
Publishing Director – Margo Embury
1150 Eighth Avenue, Regina, Saskatchewan, Canada S4R 1C9
Telephone (306) 525-2304   Fax (306) 757-2439
Email: centax@printwest.com

Dedication

This book is dedicated to my wife, Nora, without whom this and the other books we have published would not have been possible.

William H. Kelly

Deputy Commissioner Kelly, RCMP (Retired), was born in Wales, and came to Canada in 1928 at the age of seventeen. In 1933 he joined the RCMP, trained in Regina for nine months, and served five and a half years on detachments in the North Battleford sub-division of "F" Division (Saskatchewan). He spent the next six years (mostly war years) in the Criminal Investigation Branch of the "O" Division (Western Ontario), with headquarters in Toronto, where he was employed on security, sabatoge and black market activities. By 1946 he had attained the rank of Sub-Inspector. He was then posted to Personnel duties at various times in nine divisions of the Force.

In 1951 he was appointed as a liaison officer, based in London, England, to Police, Security and Intelligence agencies in Europe, and was also Officer in Charge of Visa control, supervising RCMP members employed on Immigration security in Europe in cooperation with Canada Immigration Officers. In addition, in 1952 and 1953, he was the RCMP representative at Interpol.

On his return to Canada in 1954, he supervised the enforcement of federal statutes. In 1958 he became the Assistant Director of the RCMP Security and Intelligence Directorate and in 1964 its Director. In 1959 he became the RCMP representative on the NATO Security Committee, and in 1963 he became the chairman of that committee. In 1967 he was appointed Deputy Commissioner, Operations. He retired in 1970, having served nearly 37 years in the Force. He then lectured in Criminology for two years at Ottawa University.

Since his retirement he has lived in Ottawa, and with his wife, Nora, has written several books on the RCMP and one on policing in general.

William H. Kelly & Nora Hickson Kelly

William Kelly is a former Deputy Commissioner and Director of Security and Intelligence of the RCMP. After almost forty years of service, he retired from the Force in 1970. Since his retirement he has been active as a consultant to police forces and government bodies, a university lecturer in Criminology and a writer.

Nora Kelly is a former teacher, and a noted historian of the RCMP. She is the author of *The Men of the Mounted*, and co-author, with her husband, of *The Royal Canadian Mounted Police: A Century of History,* and *Policing in Canada*. The Kellys live in Ottawa.

**Previous Books by William H. Kelly
and Nora Hickson Kelly**

- *The Men of the Mounted*, Nora Kelly

- *The Royal Canadian Mounted Police: A Century of History*, Nora and William Kelly

- *Policing in Canada*, William and Nora Kelly

- *The Horses of the Royal Canadian Mounted Police: A Pictorial History*, William and Nora Kelly

- *The Mounties: As They Saw Themselves*, William Kelly

- *The Queen's Horse: Gift of the Mounties*, Nora Hickson Kelly

- *The Musical Ride of the Royal Canadian Mounted Police*, William Kelly and Nora Hickson Kelly

The Kelly Trilogy

A personal and private look at the men in the RCMP, their training and their service, and the women who support, put up with and love them; Bill and Nora Kelly's stories are revealing and fascinating. This exceptional couple are superb examples of the men and women who helped shape both the Force and the country.

POLICING THE FRINGE: A YOUNG MOUNTIE'S STORY

From 1933 to 1939, Bill Kelly trained and was stationed with the RCMP in Saskatchewan. During frontier postings, with patrols on horseback and no telephone, he dealt with bootleggers, illicit stills, cattle and horse theft and insanity. He patrolled on horseback, by democrat, canoe, snowshoes, police car and float plane. Hardship and adventure, life in a pioneer land – the daily routine of a frontier RCMP constable, the specific and absorbing details of Bill and Nora Kelly's fine book brings this time period alive.

POLICING IN WARTIME: ONE MOUNTIE'S STORY

While Canadian service personnel made heroic sacrifices battling the Nazis, other Canadians on the home front were sabotaging the war effort. Bill Kelly, as part of the RCMP Black Market Squad in Toronto, investigated and prosecuted black market activity and security risks in southern Ontario during World War II. Bill Kelly, Former Deputy Commissioner and Director of Security and Intelligence of the RCMP, and co-author Nora Kelly's accurate account of this time period deals with blackmail, fraud, spies, sabotage, illegal gold exports, foreign exchange, gasoline and other rationing abuses. These offences and subsequent RCMP investigations were repeated throughout Canada during the war.

MY MOUNTIE AND ME: A TRUE STORY

Nora Hickson Kelly married a man, not the Force – or so she thought! At times the RCMP became a demanding third partner in the Kelly marriage. One woman's story, Nora Kelly's book details the experiences of many RCMP wives. A determined and talented writer, Nora became a freelance journalist. Her inside knowledge of the RCMP made her the ideal author and co-author of several books on the Force. Her keen observations and astonishing memory make her writing true and vital. This important book provides a glimpse into the lives of the Kellys and of many wives and their mounties.

Introduction

Much has been written about the trials and tribulations arising from World War II, mostly, and rightly so, about the activities of Canadians in uniform at home and abroad. The battles in which they were involved were matters of life and death. But while they were fighting in order to keep Canada, and other countries, from falling under the heel of Nazi Germany, there were those on the home front who were sabotaging the war effort.

The amount of certain foods, such as meat, butter and sugar were in short supply, due not only to the demands overseas, but the difficulty of producing the normal peacetime supplies. Similarly, other consumer goods such as gasoline, tires and cars were also in short supply. Hence the need for rationing and restricted purchases on items only required periodically, such as tires and cars, used and new. In addition the government decided to control the use of other products by the manufacturing industries, such as wool cloth, machine tools and scarce metals, to ensure that their use was directed to the war effort.

The government put a freeze on prices and wages in order to be able to control inflation, to avoid the situation that had arisen during World War I. During that war the rate of inflation had risen to sixty-five per cent. During World War II, these measures enabled the government to keep the rate of inflation at only three per cent.

The government established a Commodity Prices Stabilization Corporation to deal with problems arising from the importation of goods from countries where the sale of goods was not subject to any price ceiling. To allow importing manufacturers to keep the prices of their products at the ceiling prices set by the government, subsidies were paid to them, but only after their claims for subsidies had been investigated. Not a few claimants were found to be claiming subsidies where they were knowingly not warranted.

Another very important organization within government was the Foreign Exchange Control Board. Its responsibility was to ensure that money or any property exported from Canada did not detract from Canada's ability to acquire Foreign Exchange, particularly U.S. dollars, which Canada needed so badly to purchase war supplies.

The organization within government concerned with the rationing of consumer goods was the Wartime Prices and Trade Board. It established regional offices throughout Canada to deal with local problems arising from the administration of its regulations, often the prosecution for infringement of them. The Board included numerous

Administrators, mostly dollar-a-year men (volunteers).

The organization responsible for supervising the use of materials in war industries, some of which were used by consumers, such as cars, gasoline and tires, was the Wartime Industries Control Board (WICB). It had its own regulations and Controllers, also one-dollar-a-year men (volunteers).

In each region an enforcement director was appointed, usually a lawyer. It was up to him to enforce both sets of regulations through the use of civilian inspectors, mostly men and women whose jobs had become redundant because of the war. They were mainly sales people and others from business and industry whose products and services were generally unnecessary in time of war.

It was perhaps to be expected that, when there was a shortage of certain goods, many people would try to get more than their share. Hence the need for rationing. This did not stop people from trying to get more rationed products than those to which they were legally entitled, even if it meant breaking the law. This created a black market.

If only a few people had broken the law no great harm would have been done, but when the practice spread throughout society it endangered the whole purpose of rationing – a fair distribution of the goods available.

The enforcement directors found that their civilian inspectors lacked the experience to enforce the regulations adequately, so members of the RCMP were called upon to deal with matters that could only be dealt with effectively by the way of prosecution.

This book is mainly about the black market in southern Ontario during World War II, mostly in Toronto and environs, and the manner in which the RCMP Black Market Squad dealt with it. While this book deals mainly with the black market in that area, it can be safely assumed by the reader, on the word of the authors, that the same conditions prevailed all over Canada, but perhaps not to the same extent as in the heavier populated areas of southern Ontario and Quebec, and particularly Toronto. An acquaintance of the author, who was entering his teens in 1942, recalls that while living in Quebec two often-used phrases entered his vocabulary – fifth column and black market.

The black market not only consisted of those who gave food coupons from their own supply to relatives or neighbors, or who loaned a gasoline ration book to a friend to obtain more gasoline than his own ration book allowed, but also those who, in all spheres, dealt in the black market commercially.

The efforts of the RCMP black market squad in Toronto were generally aimed at the latter. As far as can be recalled, seldom was a person in the former category prosecuted. This is not to say that individuals were not prosecuted, but those who were, and there were many, were involved in some way with a commercialized black market. In fact, the RCMP Black Market Squad of ten to twelve men were so busy investigating this aspect of the black market that it had little time to deal with any other. Even at that these men knew that they were only "scratching the surface".

A few of the early stories in the book, in which the principal author was involved, are not related to the war, but happened during that period after war was declared known as the "phoney war". This was when Canada and Allied countries were hastily preparing for the time when the real war would begin. The book deals mainly with the black market activity, throughout the war, of people who cared little about the sacrifices being made by Canadian service personnel.

The contents of this book cover incidents that occurred in central Canada and the work of the group of RCMP members in Toronto, known as the Black Market Squad. It was probably more active than members of the RCMP employed on similar work in other parts of Canada. There was no doubt, however, that in proportion to the population there was as much abuse of wartime regulations in other parts of Canada as in Ontario and Quebec.

William H. Kelly
Nora Hickson Kelly

Appendices

Three appendices relating to the RCMP, court rules and the justice system are included at the end of this book as follows:

Appendix I:
Undercover RCMP Work – page 178

Appendix II:
The Rule of Silence – page 182

Appendix III:
The Philosophy of the Royal Canadian Mounted Police – page 186

ONE

After serving six years in Saskatchewan, most of them on rural RCMP detachments, I applied for a transfer to the RCMP's "O" Division, which covered western and northern Ontario and had its headquarters in Toronto. I requested it in August 1939, about a month before the beginning of World War II.

On October 16, 1939, six weeks after the beginning of World War II, I was paraded before "O" Division's CIB officer, Inspector William Schutz. I had served under him for a few weeks in 1934 in Regina Town Station detachment, immediately after graduating from the training depot. He was a pleasant and kindly man, although he had a reputation of being a Criminal Code "crank". That point did not bother me: after studying the Criminal Code for five years on detachments, I was a bit of a crank myself.

What I didn't know as I faced Inspector Schutz, was that he already knew the contents of my personal file. It had been sent to him ahead of me, and had informed him that I had conducted many criminal investigations, and had prosecuted many charges arising from them.

"You'll be going to the CIB, Kelly," Inspector Schutz said, after welcoming me to the division. I was pleased to be detailed to a position where I could continue to investigate crime, rather than to some routine job in uniform. This did not mean immediate appointment to the rank of detective constable, however, but only that I would be a "plainclothes" man, with a plainclothes allowance of twenty-five cents a day. In effect I, like others of similar status in the CIB, was on probation.

The inspector pressed a button on his desk and I soon was being introduced to Sergeant "Max" Veitch, the NCO in charge of the CIB investigators. Before long I discovered that he was sincere, fair and helpful. The sergeant gave me my first assignment, to conduct a few routine inquiries. He also gave me several "mug shots". They were of men, mostly from Western Canada, on whom arrest warrants had been outstanding for some years. Finally he gave me some streetcar tickets.

"You'll get to know the city better by traveling this way," he said.

I could see that the inquiries, most of which centred on information wanted by other Divisions of the RCMP, would need no particular police experience. Nevertheless, I appreciated them as a means of becoming acquainted with a large city, the first I had lived in.

As I made my first patrol by streetcar, I smiled as I remembered my earlier means of transportation. I had patrolled on foot, by snowshoes, by dog team, by saddle horse, by team and democrat (an oversized buggy), by team and cutter (sleigh), by team and wagon, by canoe (paddle and outboard motor), by private car (my own 1928 Ford Roadster), police car and float plane. Now I was patrolling by streetcar but, I hoped, only temporarily.

About a week later, I was sitting in a northbound streetcar on Yonge Street when I thought I recognized the man opposite me. I was about to ask him if we had met before, when I realized he might be a man in a "mug shot" I carried in the briefcase resting at my feet. With whatever slight nonchalance I could muster, I picked up my briefcase and checked the photographs.

The man opposite me certainly resembled the man in one photograph, but he differed enough for me to be doubtful. On the other hand, although the man I was looking at was older and dressed differently from the man in the "mug shot", that photograph had been taken some years before. When he got off the streetcar, so did I. And thus began my first "tailing" job.

My "quarry" transferred to another streetcar at St. Clair Avenue. I didn't yet know the transfer system so I used another streetcar ticket to follow him. After what seemed like several miles he got off. With me a discreet distance behind him, he walked a few blocks, then entered a house. I wondered if I should follow him indoors and question his identity. Instead I went to the nearest pay phone and called Sergeant Veitch, who promised to join me as soon as possible.

I kept an eye on the house to make sure my "quarry" did not

leave, and when Veitch arrived we went inside. We discovered that the man I had followed was wanted for a bank robbery in western Canada. Veitch seemed as pleased with my first tailing job as I was. He couldn't remember when any other of the "mug shots" he had given out had resulted in an arrest. As for me, I knew the arrest had been fortuitous, but it made me think that doing police work, even when traveling by streetcar rather than police car, was not so bad after all.

To my surprise, a few days later Inspector Schutz called me into his office and congratulated me. I knew I had done much better work back in Saskatchewan, without any comment from anyone, but it was good to know what I had done was appreciated, and on such a high level.

Whether it was the result of the arrest or not, the sergeant now began to give me investigations of cases that might result in prosecutions. The first arose from a letter forwarded by the U.S. Secret Service in Washington, D.C. to the RCMP. The letter had been written by a Toronto man to an American company, asking it to supply him with materials that indicated he might be involved, or hoped to become involved, in the counterfeiting of paper money. On the basis of the man's letter I obtained a search warrant and went to his address to question him, and to search his house if necessary.

The man admitted having written the letter but denied that he intended to do anything illegal. Nevertheless I searched his house. In the basement I found two large lithographing stones, and a wooden frame holding a new, uncreased, ten dollar bill. I had never seen lithographing stones before, but I knew they were used to print on paper, although I didn't know how. Seeing the ten dollar bill protected as it was by the frame, however, I suspected that the printing of money was involved.

I doubted that I had enough evidence to charge the man, a bachelor and a comparatively recent immigrant from eastern Europe, with the offence of knowingly having in his possession instruments for making paper money. What I needed was an expert lithographer to advise me. I soon found him: Mr. George Brigden of Brigden's Lithographing Company on University Avenue. He told me that an experienced lithographer could make counterfeit money with what I had found, plus a few more materials that could easily be acquired locally. He agreed to appear as a witness in court to give evidence to that effect.

If I had had this case in Saskatchewan, I would have made out a charge, sworn to it before a J.P., arrested the suspect and prosecuted him before a police magistrate. If necessary I would have taken him to jail, a hundred miles away or more. By contrast, in Toronto I discussed the case with the Toronto Crown Attorney in his office in the old City Hall. Then he prepared the appropriate written charge. It was understood that he would prosecute the case when it came to court. I took the charge to an office down the hall and swore to it before a Justice of the Peace, Mr. C.V. Linn, who then issued an arrest warrant.

At the trial, which took place in a courtroom across the hall from the Crown Attorney's office, I was the first witness. I gave evidence about finding the stones and the ten dollar bill in the accused's possession, and about his admission that he had written the letter to the company in the United States. I entered the stones, the frame containing the ten dollar bill, and the letter as exhibits.

The magistrate accepted Mr. Fred Brigden, a rather "crusty" elderly gentleman, as an expert in his field. Then Mr. Brigden stated that anyone with experience could make counterfeit paper money by using the stones and the ten dollar bill. Thus ended the Crown's case. Defence counsel cross-examined Brigden and raised doubts that counterfeit money could be made from a couple of stones and a ten dollar bill.

Brigden took offence at having his professional opinion questioned and snapped at the defence counsel, "If I could get Ottawa's approval I could use the stones, the uncreased ten dollar bill and a few materials obtained locally, and make money-makers in Ottawa look like a bunch of amateurs."

The accused did not give evidence and the magistrate sentenced him to six months in jail.

There was nothing exceptional about the case. In fact it had taken no great effort on my part, and it received some publicity. But I was pleased that my first investigation in my new Division had ended successfully.

Although I had enjoyed prosecuting in Saskatchewan, I realized that turning the matter over to a Crown Attorney saved a lot of work. Also, instead of my spending several days taking a convicted prisoner to jail, the court constable directed him downstairs to the basement cells from which someone would later take him to jail. I liked this system.

Something else was very different from Saskatchewan. Although I had arrested and prosecuted dozens of people in that province, I had never been stationed in a place big enough to have a daily paper, so I had never had my name in a newspaper. But in Toronto nearly all my court cases were reported in at least two of the three local dailies. Moreover, the Toronto reporters were seldom satisfied to report merely from court proceedings, but sought additional information, which I usually provided. In spite of their diligence I was amazed at how frequently they reported incorrectly on some aspect of even a minor case. I also found that if a prosecution reflected adversely on one of the newspapers' major advertisers, which it sometimes did, the reported case always contained a misspelling of the convicted person's name and the name of the advertiser was omitted.

I came to admire one *Globe and Mail* reporter although I never met him. He always telephoned me personally to ask if I had anything for him. I would give him the results of court cases and others we planned to prosecute. He reported everything correctly. I seem to remember that his name was McGillicuddy and I got to the point of calling him "Mac". A year or two later "Mac" assisted me in a number of federal prosecutions arising out of wartime regulations. If I thought the Wartime Prices and Trade Board in Ottawa was holding up approval for a prosecution due to political pressure, I would ask "Mac" to query the local director of the Board as to the standing of the case. Invariably approval for prosecution came along within a day or so.

The first year I was in Toronto, little of the work I did had anything to do with the war. I did, however, as did many other CIB members, after the federal government declared the Communist Party of Canada illegal, help the RCMP Special Branch seek out leading Communists who had gone underground, for whom warrants for internment existed.

An important fact in the background of the Communist situation was the non-aggression pact signed on August 23, 1939, between Hitler and Stalin. In this pact the two leaders agreed not to attack each other, and to remain neutral in case either Germany or the U.S.S.R. became involved in a war with a third country. Because of that agreement, members of the Canadian Communist Party brought their propaganda machine into full play. They denounced the "Imperialist" war against Nazi Germany. They appealed to Canadians to force the government to withdraw from the war, and they urged members of the armed forces to desert. The federal government believed that the most important party members were too dangerous to be allowed to continue their subversive and disruptive tactics. Although many of them were ordered to be interned, a number of the leading Communists went undercover and were never found. Later, when Germany and the Soviet Union were at war they reappeared and worked diligently for the Allied cause. The government had declared the Communist Party illegal, so these same people formed another communist party and named it the Labour Progressive Party, under which name they operated for some years.

Declaring the party illegal did not prevent the Communists from spreading propaganda against the war effort, through their daily newspaper and through several "front" organizations operated by secret Communist Party members or left-wing non-Communists under the direction of the Canadian Communist Party. That party took its propaganda lead from the Communist Party of the Soviet Union.

The propaganda called for the general public to demand that the government take Canada out of the war. Party members distributed pamphlets near army bases, urging members of the armed services to desert. Some members of the Communist Party were also known to have enlisted for the purpose of causing disaffection among servicemen. These were matters of concern for the RCMP Special Branch, but only of passing interest to members of the Criminal Investigation Branch, until an incident arose requiring its assistance. Canadians in southern Ontario began hearing Communist propaganda transmitted by way of random clandestine radio broadcasts.

The Special Branch, with the aid of the federal department of communications, using special equipment, were able to find the general area from which the broadcasts emanated. While these areas were being searched, the broadcasting equipment was being moved to other areas, sometimes a hundred miles away. Now the Special Branch asked for some CIB members (of whom I was one) to help in the searches. Still the broadcasts continued. It was clear, however, that those responsible for the broadcasts were closely associated with the Communist Party of Canada.

When the searchers began to doubt that they would ever catch the broadcaster, quite unexpectedly, and from an unexpected source, the RCMP received information from a woman librarian at the main library on College Street in Toronto. She gave the RCMP a notebook which had been left on a library table. It had entries indicating certain subversive activities, including radio broadcasts. The notebook contained the address of a house in the eastern part of the city.

Immediately a small group of investigators, of whom I was one, went to the address written in the notebook. The very belligerent resident could only watch as the police searched the house, without finding anything incriminating. But in the garage at the back of the house was a small van containing the broadcasting equipment. The van was owned by the person living in the house. He objected to being arrested and struck the nearest policeman with a piece of wood, opening a gash on his head.

At this point CIB assistance was no longer required and so I returned to my regular duties while the Special Branch proceeded with the prosecution. Later, the accused man was found guilty and sentenced to a prison term.

Communist propaganda against the war effort, demanding that Canada withdraw from the war, continued until the Nazis invaded the Soviet Union in 1941. Overnight, the Canadian Communist party's propaganda urged Canada to increase its war effort. Their "imperialist war" became a war for democracy, and they no longer called upon servicemen to desert. At that point no more ardent supporters of Canada's war existed than members of the Communist Party and their left-wing adherents. Those who had gone underground to avoid internment, when the party was declared illegal, now surrendered, offering to support the war effort. Soon they demanded a "second front", which continued until "D" day on June 6, 1944, when the Allies invaded Europe by way of Normandy beaches.

Meanwhile, many Italian Canadians, impressed by the Fascist Mussolini, were indicating their disloyalty to the Allied cause. The Special Branch had listed the leaders among them. When the government ordered their arrest, CIB members, including me, again assisted the Special Branch. The suspects were held in custody pending internment hearings before special Boards. Those whose behaviour indicated they could not be trusted were interned. Others were set free. I began to feel that I was more useful to the country than if I had stayed in faraway Saskatchewan.

During this same period I helped the federal Department of Immigration deal with American "stockbrokers" working out of Bay Street "boiler rooms". They formed so-called mining companies on the basis of various "moose pastures" or "dry" holes in northern Ontario and Quebec. Operating from banks of telephones in back rooms of Bay Street offices, they telephoned people all over the North American continent, and as far distant as Europe. They advised those people of mining stocks which had great potential for appreciation, and which were selling for mere pennies. By "wash trading" (supposedly selling and buying shares among themselves), they gradually boosted the price of the stocks. Thus they were able to "prove" to the people they telephoned that they could make money by buying the stocks, even at the current higher prices.

Thousands of people followed the advice of the promoters. Then when the latter believed the time appropriate, they stopped trading in the stocks. The prices dropped and the investors had only a lot of worthless paper. The "con" men then continued with newly-formed worthless companies. The many "suckered" investors complained to the Ontario Securities Commission, but it seemed unable to help them. Hence the appeal to the federal Department of Immigration, and the latter's appeal to the RCMP for help.

My work on behalf of that department consisted of getting information to supplement what the department already held on the Americans, all of which would be used as a basis for deportation proceedings. Eventually, when the Americans learned that the department was about to hold such proceedings, one by one they left Canada with their ill-gotten gains. Unfortunately, equally smooth-tongued Canadians then took over the profitable but "slimy" business.

I had been in the Criminal Investigation Branch only a month or two when Sergeant Veitch turned over to me what he termed "one of my continuing cases". It was to be one of mine until it ended in the Supreme Court of Ontario in December 1941.

It concerned the complaints of a woman named Sophie Kohen. She had a company called the Royal Canadian Coal Company but there was no evidence that she had ever sold any coal. In her lengthy telephone calls I got an idea that she thought the Royal Canadian Mounted Police was in some way interfering with her coal business by stealing her customers. At times she claimed she was being followed by men in disguise who, she said, were members of the RCMP.

In addition, she complained that letters addressed to her at the Terminal A post office, at Front and Bay Streets, were being stolen. As the postal inspectors, to whom she had complained, produced no results, she believed the RCMP should conduct an investigation. Veitch had spoken to the inspectors and had decided there was no basis for her complaint, that it was simply an obsession. The same conclusion had been arrived at in the coal business complaint.

Miss Kohen (as we always respectfully referred to her) was in her fifties. She had red hair, unnatural in its brilliance, and she always carried a full shopping bag which she claimed contained her business records. This I gathered from our telephone conversations, because she never visited our office. She appeared to visit the post office at Terminal A every day, although there were several post offices between her home in northwest Toronto and Terminal A where she could have done her business, if indeed she had any to transact. It was my job to deal with her telephone calls, and the complaints which had already been investigated and found to be without substance.

Her telephone calls were so frequent and so long that, finally, I let her talk away with the open telephone on my desk. Every once in a while I would pick it up, say "Yes, Miss Kohen," and put it down again. I then returned to whatever desk work I had to do. I doubt if she ever suspected what I was doing. When I wasn't in the office when she called, she would keep calling until I was there. There was nothing I could do but keep her happy by allowing her to talk as long as she liked on the phone.

But there came a time when she was not satisfied with the way I was handling her case, so she called RCMP commissioner S.T. Wood in Ottawa personally, in the middle of the night. I knew nothing about this until instructions arrived from the commissioner's office in Ottawa.

The commissioner wanted Miss Kohen to be advised that she was not to call him at any time, and that she should make her complaints to the Toronto office. He also wanted a report to show that this had been done. Naturally, I was the one to tell her. It was the only time, up until then, that I had met her face to face.

I passed the commissioner's message on to her and was not surprised at her reaction. She said, in effect, that I should tell the commissioner that, as long as the taxpayers of Canada paid his salary, she would call him at any time of the day or night. For us in the lower ranks the commissioner was on the right hand of God. No one should talk to the commissioner like that, even by way of a messenger. But he had asked for a report when she had been given his message. So I reported her reaction and quoted verbatim, not without some glee. I never found out if the message had the desired effect or not.

For some time after that I received no calls from Miss Kohen. I thought the commissioner's message had had some effect. It did. But not the way I had envisioned. One morning Veitch and I learned that Miss Kohen had begun proceedings in the Supreme Court of Ontario, charging that we were interfering with her social and business life and asking for $10,000 in damages. She was acting on her own behalf.

We believed that because this was the case, the employees at the appropriate court office had assisted her in making out the necessary documents. But after my interview with her, I was willing to believe that she had more ability than the average person to deal with such matters. For all we knew she might have had some legal training.

We obtained the services of Mr. T.N. Phelan, a well-known counsel, to represent us. He dealt with the matter initially, and conveyed to us his view that the case was more or less concluded, as far as the court was concerned. Later, much to our surprise, we were informed that we were to appear in the Supreme Court of Ontario, in December 1941, exactly two years after Sergeant Veitch had handed me the "Kohen case". Miss Kohen still had no counsel, and Mr. Phelan advised that as far as he knew she would conduct the prosecution herself.

She gave her evidence, and it was clear that the judge was giving her all the leeway he could in the absence of a prosecuting lawyer. At times it was quite farcical, as she argued with him about the steps he suggested she take. But the case proceeded. On cross-examination it was not difficult for Mr. Phelan to show there was not much substance to her charges. When he came to her charge that Veitch had prowled around her house in disguise, he questioned her about how Veitch was dressed. She described a somewhat elaborate amount of clothing.

"How could you identify him?" Mr. Phelan asked.

"By his legs," she said.

"Did Veitch have any trousers on?"

She said, "Yes he did."

"Did you seen him with his pants off?"

"No", she replied.

Only Sergeant Veitch was called to give evidence. Her cross-examination of him did not do her case any good. The judge brought the matter to an end and dismissed the case.

She appealed the decision in the Appeal Court of Ontario, which confirmed the Supreme Court's decision. Then she made application to the Supreme Court of Canada. On both occasions she continued to represent herself. Despite Mr. Phelan's objection, that her charges were "frivolous and vexatious", her application was granted. I never heard whether she actually appeared in the Supreme Court of Canada, and I never heard any more about her.

Dealing with Miss Kohen had wasted many long hours, over a period of two years. It had caused some neglect of my other work, but that went with the job. Without having to deal with Miss Kohen, I had enough work to do dealing with complaints in which there was some real substance. Complaints which arose from a mentally deranged person I could do without.

TWO

DuDuring the first year of World War II, before the federal departments responsible for various aspects of the war effort were properly organized, the RCMP was called on to give them considerable assistance, particularly the Department of Munitions and Supply.

A request from them in April 1940 resulted in my going to Welland, Ontario, to investigate the affairs of Salem Engineering of Canada, a subsidiary of the American company, Salem Engineering of Salem, Ohio. Welland was the town after which the canal was named, and the site of a number of industries gearing up for war work.

The Department of Munitions and Supply in Ottawa had received information alleging that Salem Engineering of Salem, Ohio, had connections with Nazi Germany. Sam Keener, a German-American owned both companies. The Canadian subsidiary was operated by Mr. Wolfe and his assistant, both Americans of German extraction, and a female Canadian secretary.

As I began my investigation, I learned from the Welland Collector of Customs that the female secretary believed there was something "fishy" going on. When I interviewed her at her home she told me she suspected that the Canadian company, through Sam Keener, had links with Nazi Germany. She also said that Sam Keener had contacts in the Department of Munitions and Supply in Ottawa that were not "altogether healthy", meaning that there was a government official looking after Keener's interests.

As an agency of the American company, the Canadian one was in the business of selling industrial furnaces to new Canadian war plants, and all expanding industries. Wolfe or his assistant had to visit plants and industries to gather details of proposed production on which they based the cost for installing appropriate furnaces. In due course they would visit all the plants in Canada involved in the production of war materials, including munitions and military equipment. In so doing they would learn much about Canada's wartime production capacity. That information would be of great value to Nazi Germany.

My informant found it strange that the Canadian company was sending Salem Engineering in Ohio several extra copies of the proposals for the installation of furnaces in Canadian war plants. She became very disturbed when she read in an engineering magazine that Salem Engineering of Ohio had an office in Berlin.

Lately, she told me, the Canadian company did not send its mail to the Ohio plant by Canadian mail. Instead, one or the other of the men made regular visits to Buffalo, N.Y., to send the mail to Salem, Ohio from that point. She had overheard the two men refer to the "Canadian censor", and she reasoned that if they were on "the up and up" they should have nothing to fear from the Canadian censor. She wondered if the letters to head office contained more than the reports she had prepared. She had conveyed her suspicions to the Collector of Customs at Welland, who must have notified his superiors in Ottawa, which resulted in my visit to Welland.

Other circumstances also aroused her suspicion. Wolfe and his assistant openly declared their lack of sympathy for Canada's involvement in the war. They gave the impression that they sympathized with the Nazi cause, without actually stating so. Also, she had learned that Sam Keener, the company's American owner, was definitely pro-Nazi. There had even been a picture of Keener in *Time* magazine, showing him wearing a made-up uniform with various insignia of his own choosing on it. The picture was taken in Berlin.

The Department of Munitions and Supply knew of Keener's company in Berlin, the secretary told me. They had questioned Keener about it but he had assured them that his American company had no connections with the German company.

My job now was to find evidence showing whether or not Salem Engineering in Ohio had a continuing connection with Nazi Germany. I interviewed a number of men in Welland who knew Sam Keener. They believed that he still had an office in Berlin, and they, like the secretary, believed he was pro-Nazi. On Keener's recent visit to Welland, at a time when Hitler was blitzkrieging over Europe, he had laughed and asked some of these men if they weren't sorry they were not on the German side. On another occasion, he had hinted to the manager of the Page Hersey plant at Welland that he had placed his money "on the wrong horse". From a person who was a consultant to Keener's company in Salem, Ohio, and to a plant in Welland, I learned that Keener continued to visit Germany after the war started. As an American he could easily do so as the U.S.A. was not then at war.

Mr. Wolfe, the manager, frequently visited Salem, and upon his return always insisted that the informant send the estimates for plant furnace surveys and proposals to Salem, Ohio, in sufficient copies for them to send them to their "office abroad". The secretary found it strange that the Welland office did not receive similar correspondence from other offices.

I did not intend to interview Wolfe or his assistant until I was forced to. I was sure they would refer me to Sam Keener in Salem. From the type of questions I would ask them, they would probably conclude that my information came from their Canadian secretary, who had made her views known in the office. This could result in her being fired. It was better for me that she remain on the job. I was quite prepared to interview them later, but I didn't have to.

I learned that an executive of the Atlas Steel Company knew Sam Keener, and might have some information of value to me. He could only confirm all that I had previously heard about Sam Keener. He knew of the advertisement in the engineering magazine, of which I now had a copy, showing the address of Salem Engineering's Berlin office. But as I was leaving his office, he wondered if I had spoken to the woman who had been employed by Salem Engineering Canada for a few weeks after the company was established, just a few weeks after World War II began.

No one had mentioned her name, not even the informant, perhaps because she had been employed only for the first few weeks of the company's existence. This woman was pleased to be interviewed. She was relieved that I had come to speak to her, she said. She produced a letter with a Salem Engineering, Ohio, letterhead addressed to the Welland office. It read:

> Will you please check to see that we get the large 4 x 6 data cards on all proposals written in Canada. There should be copies of this data card for both our London and German offices, as well as for Salem, and you should probably forward at least the German cards for us to remail. You might check to

make sure these cards have been made out for all proposals so far. Also, I want to ask you again that you make sure in each instance that you make a copy for this office of all outgoing letters.
Yours truly,
(Miss) F.E. Fernengel
Sec. to Mr. Keener.

This letter was written at the same time as Keener had successfully convinced the Department of Munitions and Supply that he had no further connections with Nazi Germany.

The woman then produced a copy of an inter-office memo, signed by the same Miss Fernengel and addressed to Mr. Wolfe, the Canadian manager:

Inter-office memo: October 11th [1939]
If you go to Welland, will you please bring back a small supply of letterheads, say about 200. We are using these since the war started so as not to flaunt our Berlin office in the eyes of the Canadians.

As far as I was concerned I now had all the information I needed, and I did not think it was necessary to interview Mr. Wolfe. It seemed evident that Keener's Nazi sympathies were leading him to send the German authorities, by way of his Berlin office, all the information on Canada's capacity to make munitions that the Welland office could gather. That could amount to the total capacity of all Canada's war factories.

My report indicated that this appeared to be a clear case of industrial espionage on behalf of the Nazis. The Department of Munitions and Supply evidently agreed, because it immediately sent a memorandum to all plants in Canada making war materials, thus effectively putting Salem Engineering Canada out of business.

Salem Engineering Co. of Canada, Welland, Ontario, should not be entrusted with any work whatsoever in connection with contracts or sub-contracts having to so with supply of munitions or war materials for the prosecution of Canada's war effort . . . and that individuals employed by the company . . . be prohibited from entering your plants, or any person directly or indirectly representing Salem Engineering of Canada or Salem Engineering of Salem, Ohio . . .

Later I learned that a copy of my report had been sent to the FBI, in case they were interested in persons in the United States who might be supplying Nazi Germany with industrial information, or who might become or were already secret German agents working against the United States.

Later Sam Keener paid a visit to Ottawa to protest the above order, but to no avail. When I was again in Welland, this time on a case of suspected sabotage, I was told that, when France capitulated, Keener said to a man I became acquainted with during the Salem Engineering investigation, "Now, which company do you think we should keep, German or Canadian?" There was no doubt about where his sympathies lay.

I had been back from Welland only a few weeks when I received a call from Mr. Jim Wilson, the General Manager of the Page Hersey Company. It had a contract with the Department of Munitions and Supply for the manufacture of casings for eighteen-inch shells. Many of the casings being produced were defective. He asked if I could go to Welland as he thought it was a matter in which I would be interested. As I was not operating a private police force, I discussed the matter with Sergeant Veitch, who discussed it with Inspector Schutz. I was given permission to go to Welland.

I had met Jim Wilson during my investigation of the Salem Engineering case. He explained that the plant in which the casings were being produced was built in the early 1930s by a German company. The German foreman of the construction crew had remained in Canada after Page Hersey offered him the job of foreman in the plant.

Wilson was deeply concerned that a large percentage of the casings were defective. The finished casings should be like an elongated eighteen-inch glass tumbler, with smooth outside walls, about half an inch thick, and open at one end. It was not unusual to have defects in the cases, but this didn't matter as long as they could be machined out. But the walls of most of the present defective casings were so deeply wrinkled that, if they were machined out, the walls of the casings would be below the standard required by the government.

The company's consulting engineer, Mr. Pugh, who lived in Salem, Ohio, could not solve the problem. He and Wilson had concluded that the problem lay with the German foreman who was helping to make shells to kill Germans. They believed he was sabotaging Canada's war effort in his own limited sphere of influence.

Sabotage was certainly a police matter, but I could hardly believe that was what it was. Surely the foreman would not commit sabotage so openly. In any case, an engineer rather than a policeman should be able to solve the problem.

Jim Wilson and I went to the shed where hundreds of casings stood in rows like little soldiers. Even I could see the indents in the walls near the open end. I found it interesting when Wilson said it was normal to have some defective casings, but of late they had become excessive. Next, Wilson and I went to the building where the cases were made. He found Hans (not his real name), the foreman, standing where white-hot ingots were being placed on a twelve-to-fifteen-foot semi-circular bed, about six inches wide, along which the ingots were being rammed at great speed by a heavy steel rod. As the ingots were propelled forward they were held down by curved steel strappings, about every foot or so, until they reached the end as long cylindrical casings.

As we watched them fall off the end, I saw several with the objectionable flaws, although others were perfect. Hans told me he was worried about the flaws, and thought he knew the cause. He suggested a very simple remedy. That was to shut down production for a couple of days, and double the number of steel straps that held the ingots in place as they were rammed along the bed. This, he said, would prevent the exaggerated "wobble" that caused the flaws.

"Have you told Mr. Wilson about this?" I asked.

"Oh, yes, and Mr. Pugh." he responded. "But they won't listen to me."

I couldn't believe his answer. I discussed Hans' suggestions with Mr. Wilson and he pooh-poohed them. I told him I thought they were reasonable and worth trying. It was then that I sensed that part of the problem was that he was reluctant to shut down the plant for several days in order to make the adjustments Hans had suggested. It seemed that enough of the casings were O.K., and production was enough to keep the Department of Munitions and Supply happy.

From the police point of view I said that was not enough to keep me happy. Unless he followed Hans' suggestion, it would be wasting my time looking for other reasons. I was convinced that the answer to the problem lay in the mechanics of the operation.

Hans was very worried. He realized his delicate situation as a German and that his heavy German accent was a constant reminder to everyone. But he had become a Canadian, he said, and his children had been born here. Of course he had feelings for Germany, but he would not do anything against Canada's war effort. He found it difficult to live with the constant suspicion. If the problem wasn't corrected, as a result of his suggestion, he would have to quit his job. I told Wilson what I believed, and left Welland with him trying to make up his mind about shutting down the casings section of the plant.

A few days later, back in Toronto, I had a call from Jim Wilson. They were going to close down the plant and try out Hans' suggestion. A week later I received another call. The first of the new casings were off the line. There had been a great improvement, and although there were still some faulty ones, most flaws could be machined out. I asked how Hans felt. "Very relieved," he answered.

I wondered why men with long engineering experience had failed to realize that Hans might have been right all along. But as I mentioned earlier, every case of damage, willful or not, since the war began became suspected sabotage. Such was the atmosphere of the time.

Three

One morning in the Spring of 1940, Inspector Schutz called me to his office and told me to proceed without delay to the RCAF station at Trenton, about 100 miles east of Toronto. There, he said, was a young RCAF officer, a member of a well-known Toronto family, who was rumoured to be homosexual. In those days homosexuality was considered shameful and homosexuals were considered security risks because it was believed they could easily be blackmailed. In wartime the possibility of blackmail, especially in the armed forces, meant the possibility of useful information being given to the enemy, perhaps harming the security of the country. It was my job to find out if there was any truth to the rumours.

As I drove to Trenton on old Number 2 highway, I compared Ontario's beautiful elms and maples, and the paved highway skirting well-established farms, with the pine forests, lakes, homesteads, and the often impassable trails of northern Saskatchewan. On arriving at the RCAF station I called upon the adjutant, Flight Lieutenant Denton Massey, who knew only that the rumours about the young officer were rife. He asked me to proceed cautiously, and to give him any information I had gained before I returned to Toronto.

I replied that in order to find out anything I would have to interview the suspect's fellow officers, and that it would be impossible to keep the investigation secret, especially on an RCAF station. The adjutant gave me the impression that this was nearly enough to call the whole thing off, but he agreed rather reluctantly that I should go ahead with my investigation.

At first it was difficult to get anyone to say anything derogatory about the officer under suspicion, until I explained my interviewing technique. Which was that I would interview many officers, whether I needed to or not, so that no finger could be pointed at anyone who gave me the kind of information I was seeking. After a couple of days I was convinced there was some evidence of homosexual activity among at least two officers, including the one I had originally come to investigate.

I told Flight Lieutenant Massey what I had learned, but didn't give him the names of the officers from whom I had received information. I explained that my next step would be to interview the two officers suspected of homosexual behaviour. I could see that he wished I had not found any indication of homosexuality, even if it existed. As he said, my information made things a little awkward.

After much hesitation, Massey promised to discuss the matter with the commanding officer, and let me know when I could return to Trenton to carry out the interviews. That was the last I heard of the matter. No one ever advised the RCMP as to how the problem had been resolved. But in case the matter of security arose later, I passed a copy of my report to the RCMP Special Branch.

From the first days of the war, incidents that in peacetime would probably have been categorized as willful damage became suspected sabotage. I investigated a number of such cases which would normally have been dealt with by the local police or the Ontario Provincial Police. Because of the "sabotage" connotation they were passed to the RCMP.

One case at Honey Harbour, on Georgian Bay, arose when the Indian Affairs department believed that six outboard motors had been "sabotaged", when sugar was found in their gasoline tanks. I never learned who did it, but my inquiries pointed to some Indian youths in the area, who denied any involvement. Certainly the mischief was not the result of subversive activity.

About this time, July 1940, I had completed seven years service, the amount required to be allowed to marry. I made the usual application for permission to do so, giving the name and address of my fiancée so that the character investigation could be made, to find out if she were a "suitable person to live in government quarters". I had heard rumours that a marriage or two had been denied on this basis, but I never knew of one.

When those bureaucratic procedures had been completed, and permission was granted by the RCMP commissioner, I applied for my annual three weeks leave. I didn't expect to be granted all of it because of the pressure of increasing work. Even so, I was not prepared for it to be denied completely. I had served the required seven years, and for three years had been engaged to marry. Now it seemed I could not get any time off to do so.

A couple of days after Inspector Schutz turned down my application for leave, he called me into his office. He wanted to know how short a time I needed to get married. I was fairly hot under the collar.

"None, sir," I replied sharply, "I can get married some evening."

Eventually he granted me three days off. My fiancée, who was now in Toronto, and I spent the first day putting finishing touches to the apartment we had rented. We got married on the second day, and spent our "honeymoon" on the third day by going to see Cary Grant in a film called *My Favorite Husband*. It wasn't much of a celebration, but that was no indication of what the future would bring. We have now been happily married over fifty-nine years, and often laugh at the circumstances under which our marriage took place.

My work was now taking me all over western Ontario, from Cobourg in the east, to Windsor in the west, and to Timmins in the north. I was given another case, the break and enter of the post office in Brighton, a small town on Lake Ontario. I considered it to be, like the sugar in the gas tanks at Honey Harbour, the responsibility of the local police. I presumed the RCMP became involved because the post office was federal government property. I investigated a number of other cases with federal interests and they took me all over the division.

When working locally in the Toronto area I hardly ever got home for supper. This was the beginning of fourteen years of similar working conditions. Long hours and travel became the norm. How my wife put up with me under such conditions is a tribute to her support. But to this day she is convinced that when I married her I committed bigamy, because I was already married to the RCMP. Other members of the Force have been similarly accused.

I was fortunate in that the RCMP rewarded me with early and repeated promotion. The first came in November 1940, when I was appointed to the rank of detective constable, with its very acceptable fifty-cents-a-day detective pay. As I lost my twenty-five cents a day plainclothes allowance, however, my net gain was only twenty-five cents. This appointment was a surprise, especially as I, the most recent member of the CIB, was the only one to receive it at that time.

Meanwhile the federal government, through the Department of Munitions and Supply, had entered into numerous contracts, for the manufacture of goods and machines for the war effort, for the building of new factories, and for the expansion of old ones. The RCMP were called upon to investigate cases in which those who had entered into contracts were unable, or unwilling to fulfill them. My first such case took me to Delhi, Ontario, where a man was having difficulties in living up to his contract for the delivery of military truck bodies. The investigation showed that he had entered into a contract before he had acquired the capacity to manufacture the truck bodies.

Other investigations showed clearly that contractors had no intention of living up to their agreements. They had built factories at government expense, but failed to make the best use of them. No doubt the Department of Munitions and Supply, at the beginning of the war, had more work than it could properly handle, and had awarded contracts without ascertaining that the contracts were within the capabilities of the contractors. Contracts had been awarded without enough care being taken to show that the contractors had the facilities to fulfill them. Even fraud was evident. However, the department refused to prosecute. It became clear that all it wanted was to intimidate the contractors into returning the money advanced by the government. After a number of such investigations the RCMP made a policy that if the government did not agree to prosccute, even though evidence was forthcoming, the RCMP would refuse its assistance.

In spite of that policy, it agreed to the Department of Munitions and Supply request that a member of the Force go to the plant of the National Steel Car Company in Malton, where that company was making Lancaster bombers. The department asked only that the member observe the conditions in the plant during working hours and report. I was given the case, and told to contact the RCAF member who was stationed at the plant as the technical advisor to the company, and whose complaint had resulted in the department's request to the Force.

At the plant the RCAF member briefed me on the situation. The company had a "cost-plus" contract with the government to build Lancaster bombers. It was clear to him that the company had no desire to complete its contract within a reasonable time. The longer it was stretched out the more money it would make. He had become so frustrated with conditions in the plant that he had complained bitterly to the RCAF, who in turn complained to the Department of Munitions and Supply.

It occurred to me that the department should have sent someone better qualified than a member of the RCMP to look into the matter, although I certainly was an independent viewer as requested. I stood in the RCAF officer's office, high up in one corner of the vast plant. I could see a number of Lancaster bomber bodies in various stages of manufacture, but not even one man could be seen working on them.

All over the floor men stood in small groups, and a few others worked at their benches. Nothing indicated that this was a factory with a contract to build urgently needed bombers. The RCAF officer said that what I saw was the usual state of affairs.

The RCAF officer and I walked around the floor. I realized that it didn't take an expert in aircraft production to see what was *not* going on. According to the officer, most of the men seen on the floor made up about half of the work force. As we passed the few men at their benches, some of them pretended to be busy, not machining aircraft parts, but metal lunch boxes. Some workers on the floor appeared to be just visiting other workers at their benches. One man, carrying a hammer for some strange reason, walked around the whole floor without visiting anyone before returning to his bench.

As we came to a skeleton of a bomber high up off the ground on a holding frame, we heard the sound of hammering on metal. At least, I thought, one worker is doing something productive. But as we came abreast of him I saw I was wrong. A man was sitting on scaffolding, his feet dangling in space, and with one hand holding a wrench he was hammering rhythmically on the steel scaffolding. He didn't stop when we came into sight, and we walked away to the same steady rhythm.

I saw no one who seemed to be acting as a supervisor, and my companion said that was the case most days. We decided to visit one of the plant's several washrooms. It was so crowded that we could hardly enter. The men apparently suspected that we were not there to use the facilities. They walked out a few at a time, till eventually we were the only two left there. At least, I thought, these men had the decency to waste their time out of sight.

Obviously the company had no interest in keeping the men at work, since the cost-plus contract allowed it to make money on every non-productive hour the men spent in the plant. Perhaps the cost-plus system was the only practical way of gearing up Canada's war effort. But considering the hundreds, perhaps thousands, of similar contracts throughout Canada for the building of ships, planes and other war materials, the cost to the taxpayers must have been unconscionably exorbitant. Even so, the Department of Munitions and Supply had yet to appoint their own inspectors to supervise the countless contracts into which they had entered.

I had not been required to interview anyone except for the RCAF officer, in order to obtain an explanation for the conditions I had observed at the plant. I was required only to observe and report. My report criticized not only the company but also the Department of Munitions and Supply for allowing such conditions to exist at public expense. I heard no more about the matter. But often during the next year or two I frequently passed the plant. Eventually I saw flags, each with a large "E" for excellence, flying from the factory rooftops. I wondered how deserved they were. However, a few months after my visit I saw Lancaster bombers being tested near the plant. I hoped my report had contributed something to the war effort.

One feature of my work during the first year of the war was the variety of cases I handled. Illustrative of this was the case in which it was suspected that matters were not all they should be within the parimutuel betting area at the Hamilton, Ontario, racetrack. Federal interest arose from the fact that there was a federal tax on the betting "take" on each race. An RCMP squad of four or five men supervised the operation of the betting wickets, and collected the government's tax at the end of each day's racing, as well as urine samples from the winning horses. These samples were taken to a federal government laboratory each evening to be tested for illegal stimulants.

Suspicion was aroused when someone reported to the federal Department of Agriculture, the department responsible for supervising racetracks, that on a certain race at Hamilton, the *last* ten tickets had been torn all at once from a ten-dollar ticket pad of the winning horse, Kinsail. It was unusual that one person had purchased the last ten, ten-dollar tickets on a winning horse. It was even more unusual that the tickets had been cashed at the main cashier's wicket inside the betting area, to which the public did not have access, rather than the usual public bet-paying wickets. The cashing of winning tickets at the main cashier's wicket was against the rules.

The RCMP had the responsibility of ensuring that the betting wickets were closed just before a race started, and of ensuring further that the betting amounts were recorded at that time. As I made my inquiries I could see the possibility of neither being done on time. Nor had the member recording the amount of bets at the ten-dollar wicket noticed that the last ten-dollar tickets had been torn off the pad all at once, and in some haste. Because my investigating took place a few weeks after the race, it was easy for the RCMP squad, the parimutuel employees, the ten-dollar ticket seller, and the chief cashier to blame their inadequate answers on memories. There was no doubt, however, that supervision by the RCMP squad had become lax.

The lax supervision could have made it possible for the ten-dollar ticket seller to have torn the ten tickets off the pad before the RCMP had recorded the sales on the Kinsail race, toward the end of the race. The ticket seller could have known by way of the loud speaker system that, near the end of the race, Kinsail was so far ahead of the other horses that he was bound to win. Because his sales had not been recorded soon enough, the ticket seller would feel safe in taking the ten tickets off the pad and putting $100 in his cash. That these particular tickets were cashed with the chief cashier, inside the betting complex, and against the rules, pointed to the ticket seller and the inside cashier being involved in a scheme to make easy money.

When I questioned the ticket seller and the chief cashier, both insisted the incident had taken place too long ago for them to remember it. The RCMP members denied leaving the recording of ticket sales late enough to allow the ticket seller to take advantage of it. But I felt sure that the tickets would only have been torn off before sales had been recorded, when Kinsail appeared to be a sure winner. I showed both the ticket seller and the chief cashier the ten, ten-dollar tickets, which had parts of the stubs attached, clearly indicating that they had been torn off in some haste, and all at once. But both claimed they could not remember handling them, although the chief cashier, facing something he could not deny, admitted cashing the tickets.

The fact that the tickets had been cashed inside the betting complex clearly showed that the tickets were cashed by an employee, and the logical suspect was the ten-dollar ticket seller. It was reasonable to believe that at least these two men had cooperated in a scheme to defraud the parimutuel system. I could only wonder how many times such efforts had been successful.

I believed I had enough evidence to warrant the prosecution of the two men, and placed the facts before Mr. John J. Robinette, then legal advisor to the RCMP. He thought not, so no charges were laid. Even so, the two employees were dismissed, and the RCMP supervisor was replaced. I recommended that supervisors be changed periodically, to ensure that members of the racetrack detail would not get too friendly with parimutuel employees, and that they would carry out their duties strictly according to the rules. These recommendations were accepted and another case went into the files.

This was the first of many cases that indicated to me that the special counsel, appointed by the federal government to prosecute our cases, insisted on an overwhelming amount of evidence before they would recommend prosecutions. No doubt their attitude in most cases was the result of their lack of experience in prosecuting criminal cases, as many of them were prosecuting such cases for the first time. I believe that we RCMP investigators led most of them to overcome their reluctance.

Soon after the racetrack investigation, and before the amalgamation of the Imperial Bank with the Canadian Bank of Commerce, I was given a case that involved the forging of Imperial Bank money orders. As a Criminal Code offence it should have been handled by the Toronto City police. I suspected I was asked to investigate because Sergeant Veitch and the bank's chief inspector had worked on such cases over the years, and because the RCMP were considered responsible for matters involving counterfeit money. The chief inspector had acquired a number of raised money orders from two east-end Toronto branches of the bank. They had originally been purchased for ten dollars each at two west-end branches, and this amount had been raised to seventy dollars.

The forgery was so cleverly done that it was not until the main bank's accounting system revealed the discrepancies that the bank was aware of it. I made inquiries at the selling banks and obtained a vague description of the suspect. He was a young man, about 20 years of age. I gave his description to the cashing banks, hoping that some alert teller would recognize him, if not by the description, by the amount of the money order he was cashing. I also told the managers of these banks to hold anyone they suspected of cashing forged money orders, and to call the local police station.

The forging and uttering continued, but the amounts involved became greater. No doubt the forger was gaining confidence in his ability to pass the forged money orders. After a few weeks the bank inspector telephoned to tell me that a young man was being held at an east Toronto branch of the bank. The chief inspector and I went there immediately.

We found a well-dressed young man with a shock of blonde hair sitting in the manager's office. We used a magnifying glass to check the money order he had tried to cash. We saw that it had been tampered with. I placed the young man under arrest, and took him to my office where I took a written statement from him. I learned that his father was an executive of Neilson's Chocolates in Toronto's west end.

Before I left the office to take the prisoner to the city police holding cells, the bank inspector telephoned to ask if the young man would show him how he raised the money orders. Quite willing to do so, the prisoner accompanied me to the inspector's office in the head office of the bank on Bay Street. The bank's cheques and money orders were of a pink shade and, in preparation to raise the money order, he simply soaked a blank pink cheque in some water to make some "paint". Then he erased the original single figure one from the ten-dollars, and used the paint to hide the erasure. Next he skillfully inserted the figure seven.

"I could do a better job if I had my own tools," he said.

I took him to the city police cells. He was soon released on bail by his father, whom we had notified of his son's arrest. The next morning, charged with forgery and uttering, and represented by a lawyer, he appeared before a magistrate who remanded his case for a week. I was sure that at the next hearing the young man would plead guilty to the charge, as the evidence against him was ample. But before the next hearing the bank inspector telephoned to ask if I could visit his office. Shamefacedly he told me that something had arisen which made it difficult, if not impossible, for the bank to proceed with the charges against the young man. Evidently, this was not his idea but that of higher bank authorities. It seemed that either the youth's father or the Neilson Chocolate Company, or both, were valued customers of the bank, and that if we proceeded with the charges the bank feared it would lose valuable accounts. Moreover, the father promised to pay the bank all the money it had lost by cashing his son's raised money orders.

When I informed the Crown Attorney of the situation, he said he was familiar with such charges being withdrawn. However, I did think that the investigation was worthy of a more satisfactory ending. I did not particularly want to see the youth go to jail, but the extent of his criminal behaviour warranted a criminal conviction, though perhaps with a suspended sentence. A conviction would at least show him the seriousness of what he had done, and would probably act as a deterrent in the future if he was tempted to repeat his undesirable activity.

FOUR

During the 1930s the federal government had enacted the Home Improvement Loans Act, aimed at easing the prevailing unemployment. Homeowners could apply through the banks for loans that would allow them to make improvements to houses they owned, including their homes. An application, supported by estimates from a contractor, was usually automatically approved, and some applicants received large sums of money. The fact that the federal government guaranteed the loans allowed banks to pay less attention to the character of an applicant than it would have done when making loans in the usual way. The lax administration of the Act left it open to general abuse.

The appropriate federal government department requested the RCMP to look into the loans granted to a Mrs. Gloria Murphy and her contractor. She resided in a large house in central Toronto, and had received a loan of $6,500 after the bank had approved her application, supported by a contractor's estimates. The contractor had also received $2,000 as a result of his application. The ease with which such loans were obtained seemed to indicate that the federal government did not expect them to be repaid. It did, however, expect that the money would be used for home improvements.

It did not take me long to find out that neither Mrs. Murphy, nor the seventy-two-year-old contractor, who seemed to be her boyfriend, had spent any money on improving the homes designated in their applications. Also, considering the lengthy period that had elapsed since they had received the loans, it seemed clear that they had no intention of doing so. In fact Mrs. Murphy had not only spent the $6,500, but also the contractor's $2,000, which she had somehow inveigled him to part with.

Mr. Jack German was appointed special prosecutor, and both Mrs. Murphy and the contractor were charged with obtaining money by false pretenses. They were also charged with conspiracy to defraud the federal government, which gave me experience in dealing with the first of many conspiracy charges during the war years.

The case was heard in the York County Court before Judge Ian McDonnell. After the Crown's case had been presented, Mrs. Murphy, who was represented by counsel and had pleaded not guilty, gave evidence on her own behalf. She said she intended to repay the loan, but had been forced to use the $6,500 to pay "pressing debts", which her left her with nothing to spend on home improvements.

By contrast the old contractor pleaded guilty. Speaking to the court before being sentenced, he said he had been prepared to do the work on Mrs. Murphy's home, but she had not been able to give him any money to carry out the proposed repairs. He explained that he had loaned his own $2,000 to Mrs. Murphy, but she had not even been able to repay it. He said he realized that he had been duped.

Before sentencing the accused, Judge McDonnell declared he was convinced that both of them had taken advantage of an easy way to obtain money, and that neither of them had any intention of repaying the loans. He took into consideration the age of the contractor and gave him a suspended sentence.

Mrs. Murphy, however, had committed previous offences. She had obtained $450 by false pretenses, although that charge had been withdrawn. She had also passed three worthless cheques, for which offences she had served ten days in jail. With her several daughters in the court, the judge now sentenced her to three years in the penitentiary.

"Yours is one of the most barefaced frauds I have ever encountered," he declared.

I expected him also to criticize the way the government administered the Act, since the Crown's evidence had shown that loans were made simply on the basis of applications for them. But the judge failed to comment on that point. However, in my conclusion of case report I mentioned that the government had invited fraud by the manner in which people were able to obtain loans.

By mid-1940 Canada was gearing up for war, and was recruiting for the armed services at a fast pace. Whenever an investigation was needed at Stanley Barracks, at the temporary barracks in the

Exhibition grounds nearby, or at Camp Borden about sixty miles north of the city, I was given the job. Later on the Military Provost Company handled its own investigations, but for the time being the RCMP lent its assistance in any suspected criminal matter. Many of my cases involved the theft of money from servicemen who had left it in their barrack rooms, and any successful investigation meant I had to return to give evidence when charges were disposed of in a military orderly room.

Theft of money was not unexpected, especially as many servicemen had been petty criminals in civilian life, and had merely changed the scene of their operations. I successfully concluded many theft of money cases when I copied the method Sergeant Veitch had used over many years. With the assistance of the servicemen from whom money had been stolen, we left some money in the place from which the first money had been taken. But I had previously sprinkled it with a powdered green dye that reacted to even the normal moisture on a person's skin and became indelible. Anyone touching the dye with his bare hands found that his hands were stained green. The more he tried to wash it off the more it spread. Any soldier found with green-stained hands had to admit that he had placed them where they should not have been. I attended two "show hands" parades, where the soldiers were instructed to show their hands. The ones with green stains were easily identified.

I handled most of these cases while I was a detective constable, and at Camp Borden I was always invited to eat in the officers' mess. As the army had no rank of constable, apparently it didn't upset the officers to allow me to mingle with them. After I was promoted to corporal, however, presumably the officers thought it beneath their dignity to have a corporal, even a police corporal in plain clothes, sitting at a table with them. They never again invited me to eat in the officers' mess.

One case at Stanley Barracks involved not the theft of money, but the theft of binoculars. Early in the war the army had put out a call to the public for the loan of binoculars. Patriotic Torontonians donated hundreds of pairs, on the understanding that when the army bought its own the loaned ones would be returned. Eventually the army had its own supply, and it was time to return those they had borrowed. Then the stores staff discovered that only about half of the borrowed binoculars remained in the army stores. Hence a call to the RCMP.

It seemed like a hopeless case. Hundreds of soldiers had passed through Stanley Barracks since the war began, and the staff in the stores had changed constantly. I tried in vain to find someone who had worked in the stores when the binoculars came in, or at some time later. All the current staff knew was that only half of the borrowed binoculars were in the stores. I gave up all hope of finding anyone who could give me useful information, but I asked the corporal in the orderly room to be on the lookout for anyone who might do so.

I called on the corporal several times without success, and then I decided to visit him for the last time. If he had nothing then, I would close the investigation "for want of information". To my surprise that next visit was not my last. Without saying a word the corporal pointed to a soldier standing on crutches at a nearby desk, and said he had worked in the stores before spending several months in hospital. It was as if someone had turned on a bright light in a very dark room.

The soldier told me the names of all those who had worked in the stores during the time he had been there. He remembered the binoculars coming in, and what was more important to me, a large number of them going out – in the possession of the men being transferred from the stores to other duties. Apparently it was the thing to do when transferred – choose a pair of binoculars and take them with you. In fact, he said, he had a pair himself. I went to his barrack room with him and retrieved them.

I gave the adjutant the names I had obtained from the soldier, and asked him to track them down through the military police. From time to time I paid him a visit and learned that dozens of pairs of binoculars were coming back into stores. Some were returned by soldiers still in Canada, but a few came from soldiers who were located in England. Eventually I could account for all but a few. I had visions of appearing in orderly rooms all over the country when charges were laid against the soldiers involved in stealing the binoculars. However, at a time when so many soldiers were being transferred from one place to another, and with so many involved, it seemed impractical to lay charges, especially as most of the binoculars had been returned.

Even after the military provost took over most of the criminal work, I continued throughout the war to visit army barracks to investigate soldiers and airmen who were dealing illegally in gasoline ration coupons, tires and other rationed goods to which they were not entitled. Many of these cases were dealt with in civil court, but some were dealt with by way of orderly room hearings by the military units concerned, all of which required my attendance as a witness.

In the late winter of 1940-41, I and two other members of the division were chosen to attend the Canadian Police College Class No 7, beginning on March 17, 1941 at the RCMP "N" Division (Training) at Rockliffe, Ontario. I was astonished to be one of the three chosen. For one thing I was a comparative newcomer to the division, with less service than many constables there. Also, many NCOs might have been chosen to attend in my place. It was a feather in anyone's cap to be chosen for such a prestigious course, the most important police training course that a member of any police force could attend in Canada, often attended by senior policemen from British Commonwealth forces.

I had been married only nine months, and did not look forward to leaving my wife behind in Toronto for three months. There was little I could do, however. To refuse to go was unthinkable. Once we accepted this, I began to look forward to the course with some enthusiasm. I had already learned that a good showing was a great advantage in an RCMP career. I had always regretted having to leave school, and when I joined the RCMP I decided to take any and every opportunity to learn whatever mattered in a police career. With this in mind I applied myself diligently to basic training, and although I had been out of school for several years, I did exceedingly well academically. I recognized the police college course as another valuable opportunity.

Arriving at "N" Division I found it was a smaller version of "Depot" Division, Regina, with its barracks, stables, administrative and other buildings. The setting differed greatly from "Depot's" bleak prairie surroundings. "N" Division, on a bank of the Ottawa River, was surrounded by green fields and well-wooded areas, some of which were cared for by federal government workmen.

The college course was heavy on practical criminal investigative methods, with just enough physical training to keep us in shape. Dr. Maurice Powers, the RCMP pathologist, took the forensic medicine lectures. He made these fascinating. I presumed that every member of the class wanted to apply his newly gained knowledge to a murder investigation the moment he returned to practical police work. I couldn't look forward to such a thing. The division in Ontario that I came from was a "federal" division. Here the enforcement of Criminal Code offences, including murder, was the responsibility of municipal or provincial police. Still, one never knew in the RCMP when one would be transferred to a division in which the RCMP had policing contracts, as in six provinces, the Yukon and the Northwest Territories. Incidentally, Dr. Powers died a few years later in a plane crash at North Battleford, Saskatchewan, after conducting a post-mortem in that city.

Forensic medicine was such an extensive subject that we received lectures on it from the beginning to the end of the course. We learned how to tell if poisoning was the cause of death and, in some cases by the discolouration of the body, what poison had been used. We were reminded that the symptoms of a suspected poisoning death could be similar to those of a disease, as with arsenic and gastritis. Certain discolourations on various parts of the body could also indicate if the body had been removed from the place where the death had occurred.

In a suicide by hanging, was it really a suicide or had the body been hung up after death in an attempt to hide a murder? Dr. Powers explained how to tell the difference. We learned about many kinds of wounds, including those caused by shooting, stabbing or blunt force. We were introduced to such subjects as sexual crimes, abortions and asphyxia.

We were told of the importance of protecting a crime scene and the need for a plan drawing for presentation in court. We were taught how to tell if a person had really drowned, or had been placed in water after death. We learned if a victim found in a fire had really been burned to death, or had been placed in the fire after having been murdered, or had been placed in a building before it was set alight.

Much more could be said about these lectures, but at least it should be noted that all cases Dr. Powers referred to were based on his experience as a pathologist in New York City.

Another lecturer covered burglary investigation. In one of these lectures we were shown how to tell from glass fractures in a window if it had been broken from the inside or the outside, indicating whether it was an inside or an outside job. We were taught how to make plaster casts of such things as footprints and tire tracks in clay, sand and even mud puddles. We learned how to record various measurements to compare the length of stride, angle of walking and so on, of foot tracks at the scene of a crime, and to compare them with those of a suspect.

Two of the most interesting subjects for me were ballistics and document examination. The ballistics expert not only dealt with identifying firearms, bullets and cartridges, but also with the identification of blunt instruments and their relation to the marks made by them on various objects. He illustrated this latter item by showing how he could identify a pair of clippers, found in the possession of a suspect, from the marks on the wire of a severed line fence. He also showed us how he could identify a pry bar from the marks on a wooden door that had been forced open by it.

The instruments most useful to a ballistics expert were micro-scopes and micrometer calipers. With these instruments, and a great deal of experience, he could identify bullets and cartridges fired from a specific firearm, and vice versa. From the ballistics expert we learned how to bring back a serial number on a firearm, obliterated in an attempt to prevent the police from tracing it to its owner. In or-der to illustrate his evidence in court, he made use of enlarged pho-tographs of his findings.

The document examiner showed us how he compared known signatures, and the writing of a forger, with the writing on docu-ments suspected of being forged. As was the case with the ballistics expert, the document examiner, too, made use of microscopes and micrometers for the purpose of comparing measurements and vari-ous characteristics of known and unknown writings. We watched as the examiner compared a typewritten letter that threatened injury to the receiver, with a document he had just typed from a typewriter found in possession of a suspect. He showed us why he believed that both had been typed on the same machine.

One important aspect of the examiner's work was the identifi-cation of counterfeit money. He, like the ballistics expert, made use of enlarged photographs to illustrate his evidence in court. Another thing they had in common was that they both spent a great deal of time traveling to and from courts in various parts of the country. During our lectures by these experts, we students realized more than ever before the value of their work to police investigators. We saw how they turned potential evidence into the real evidence required at a trial.

We were all familiar with fingerprints, having taken them quite satisfactorily from accused persons over a period of years. But on this police college course we learned the more advanced classifica-tion and retrieval of fingerprints. We were taught how to use various powders to raise fingerprints on a variety of objects. These lectures indelibly printed in our minds the importance of such fingerprint characteristics as deltas, whorls, bifurcation and other fingerprint features.

As a relief from subjects related to the gathering of evidence in the field, we had lectures on the Criminal Code. I was reasonably fa-miliar with the Code, having studied it assiduously when I was in charge of a detachment in Saskatchewan and had to prosecute my own cases. But I had no experience in prosecuting a conspiracy charge, nor had I the opportunity to study the common law which had accumulated over a century or more as a result of conspiracy prosecutions. I found it intensely interesting, and later I made good use of the knowledge gained in this area at the college.

Even more important than the Criminal Code, however, were the subjects related to the fact that Canada had been at war for about eight months. This period was often referred to as the "phony war", but it was a time when Canada and her Allies were building their strengths to meet the inevitable onslaught of the Germans on land, on the sea and in the air. We received lectures on sabotage, on bomb making, and the explosives used by saboteurs. We were lectured on subversive activities by Communists, Fascists and even Canadians of no apparent connection with these organizations.

We also learned a new term, "Civil Security". This Civil Security section of the RCMP ensured, as far as was humanly possible, that the operation of war plants, railways and power plants was free of interference by subversives and saboteurs.

Many wartime laws had been enacted, but the two that were presented to us in the class were the War Measures Act and the Foreign Exchange Control Board (FECB) regulations. The former was the law that dealt with Canada's entry into the war, and those matters from which came government authority to prosecute the war to its fullest.

The FECB regulations were enacted so that Canada could gather all the foreign exchange received by Canadians who exported goods to other countries. This applied particularly to the the huge amount of goods exported to the United States for which we received American funds. This money could then be used to purchase war supplies from the United States. During the war Canada could never have enough U.S. dollars. Some Canadian exporters, all of whom were licensed under the regulations, resented being ordered to bring their American funds back to Canada.

To ensure that they did, FECB inspectors were given very broad powers to enforce the regulations. What these civilian inspectors, mostly Bank of Canada employees, lacked was experience in criminal investigation. Hence the need for RCMP assistance when prosecutions were intended.

I became well acquainted with various wartime regulations made pursuant to the War Measures Act, and I spent much of my time during the war enforcing them. It was impossible to foresee that, within a few months of leaving the police college, I would be working on the most extensive Foreign Exchange Control Board case to arise during the war years. The knowledge gained on the course proved to be invaluable.

At the beginning of the Police College course we had been advised that we would have to take an extensive examination at the end of it. With this in mind I took copious notes throughout the course. Each evening, before going to bed, I typed the day's notes into a permanent notebook. Then I read all notes I had typed on all subjects up to the last entry.

As the course lengthened, so did the hours I spent typing and studying my notes, until toward the end of the course I was up long after midnight typing and studying. On Saturdays and Sundays I retired to a secluded spot near the barracks and studied some more. I felt confident that I would do well in the examination, and I was satisfied that no one on the course had got more out of it than I had.

At examination time I wondered if I might encounter a question I couldn't answer. Yet I did not answer all the questions. I failed to see a question my classmates saw and it was one I could easily have answered. Fortunately, in all other respects I felt I had done well.

A few weeks after my return to Toronto, the C.O., Superintendent V.A.M. Kemp, called me into his office and congratulated me on my college results. I had placed first, with an A+ and a mark of 92.5 per cent. I could only think that I would have done better if I hadn't overlooked that one question. The superintendent was very pleased, he said. I believed him, since my first place showing proved his good judgment in choosing me for the course. But the C.O. was not half as pleased as I was, or my wife, who agreed with me that the three months I had been away had been worthwhile.

For the next six years, I was promoted in some form each year but one. Each time I liked to think that it was the result of my work, and of my experience as a criminal investigator in Saskatchewan, which I was applying to my present work. But I couldn't help thinking that my showing at the college had some bearing upon it.

About the time I returned from the police college, the Royal Norwegian Air Force requested RCMP assistance in dealing with their own policing problems. Their main base was near Gravenhurst, Ontario, about 100 miles north of Toronto, and another was at Little Norway, on Toronto's lakefront. Probably my standing at the police college caused the C.O. to choose me to lecture to the Norwegian military police. Certainly the knowledge gained at the college allowed me to make my lectures interesting and informative in the matter of criminal investigation. In preparing my notes for the lectures I made good use of the extensive notes I had taken at the college. I enjoyed giving the lectures, but begrudged the time spent traveling the 200-mile return trip to Gravenhurst.

Undoubtedly, as I learned some years later, it was my showing at the police college that led the C.O. to place me on his very confidential "potential officer" list.

When I left Saskatchewan in the fall of 1939, I was sure that my asking for a transfer to Toronto to study singing, with the hope of becoming a professional singer, would surely slow my progress in the organization. Nevertheless, after doing so well at the college I began to think that perhaps I should give up the idea of being a singer.

However, when I returned to Toronto from the college I had not forgotten my desire to become a professional singer. So again I started my vocal lessons, which I took twice a week in the evenings. Even then police work often interfered, and lessons were often taken "on the run". There was no such thing as an eight-hour day, or a five-day week in those days, and certainly no thought of overtime pay.

FIVE

I had been back from the police college only a few weeks when I was loaned by the CIB to the Preventive Service (PS) branch at division headquarters. It dealt mainly with smuggling offences under the Customs Act, and the illicit distillation of alcohol under the Excise Act. These offences, like crime in general throughout Canada, had lessened considerably as more and more real and potential criminals enlisted in the armed services. When the newly formed Foreign Exchange Control Board (FECB) asked for assistance to its investigative group in Toronto, the NCO in charge of the PS branch, a staff sergeant, was given the responsibility of supervising such assistance.

The FECB investigation groups throughout Canada were formed early in the war to deal with offences under the newly enacted Foreign Exchange Control Board regulations. The Board, an adjunct of the Bank of Canada, required those regulations to ensure, among other things, that the foreign exchange acquired by any Canadian company or individual found its way into the bank's coffers.

Foreign exchange was of vital importance to Canada's war effort. It was needed to pay for war materials purchased abroad, particularly from the United States, and to pay the interest on our foreign debts. Of special importance to a country at war, it was also needed to maintain Canada's credit rating abroad.

The FECB regulations ensured that the Board had control over the system. They required all exporters of Canadian commodities of every kind to obtain licenses before being allowed to export. They placed a restriction on certain imports, a move that saved $6 million monthly in foreign exchange. They also required Canadian residents to sell their holdings of foreign exchange to the government. They imposed a ten per cent surcharge on all purchases from non-sterling countries. They denied Canadians funds for pleasure travel abroad, thus effecting a saving of from $60 to $70 million a year. The Board encouraged the importation of goods from Great Britain, so that payment could be made in sterling instead of dollars.

The Toronto civilian inspectors of the Board, however, under the supervision of Max Fell, a former Customs investigator, had soon found that the enforcement of the FECB regulations often required police investigative experience. Hence McElhone's transfer. But there came a time when the FECB investigation group required more RCMP assistance. The staff sergeant in charge of the RCMP Preventive Service Branch asked his superior, Inspector Bill Schutz of the CIB, for authority to transfer one of his men to the FECB group. Instead of granting that authority, Schutz told him, "Take Kelly from the CIB."

As the staff sergeant had good men he could have spared from his branch, he undoubtedly objected to my transfer, but was in no position to go against the inspector's instructions. He indicated his annoyance by taking it out on me. Whenever I had to report to him on an FECB matter to keep him abreast of how our work was progressing, his antagonistic manner showed clearly that I was not welcome in his branch.

Up to the time I was transferred to his branch he had always been friendly. I couldn't understand his attitude. He certainly knew that I had nothing to do with my transfer to the FECB group, and he had no reason to be antagonistic.

I put up with his attitude for a while, but one day I went into his office and closed the door behind me. He looked up from his desk and waited for me to speak.

"Staff," I said firmly, not in an unfriendly way, "I have a serious complaint to make about the treatment I am receiving from an NCO."

"Who is the NCO?" he asked, leaning back in his chair. I was sure he thought I was referring to one of the several NCOs in his branch.

"You," I answered.

He looked shocked, and asked me to explain. After giving him specific examples of his unjustifiable antagonism, I told him that I couldn't take any more of it. If it continued I would have to request my return to the CIB, and if I were asked for my reasons, I would give the same reasons I had just given him.

The staff sergeant turned in his chair and looked out at the busy traffic on Front Street. He remained motionless for several minutes, long enough to make me think he had forgotten I was in the room, or that he was continuing the treatment I had complained about. But I knew he must have realized that if indeed I did request a return to the CIB, it would be embarrassing for him. I also knew it was rumored that he would soon be commissioned as a sub-inspector, and he would not want a complaint such as mine on his record. After about five minutes, although it seemed longer, he turned to face me again.

"You need have no further worries," he said at last. "There'll be a change." He kept his promise.

About six years later, after the staff sergeant had become an inspector, and was the senior personnel officer of the RCMP, I, too, had been commissioned and was a sub-inspector. As the divisional personnel officer for four divisions of the Force, I was subordinate to him, with an office next to his at RCMP headquarters in the Justice Building in Ottawa.

It was his responsibility to make confidential annual reports on his half-dozen divisional personnel officers stationed throughout Canada. Remembering our clash in Toronto some years earlier, I wondered what kind of report he had put in on me. Quite improperly I persuaded his NCO clerk to show it to me. It was very fair and I could not complain. But I smiled as I read his final sentence. "He does not suffer fools gladly," he had written.

I wondered if he had been thinking of himself, and the day in his office when I told him that unless there was a change in working conditions I would ask to return to the CIB. In any case, it was true that I did not suffer fools gladly. I still have not overcome that trait.

The FECB case that required extra police assistance arose from the high-grading conspiracy of stealing gold from gold mines, and committing the crimes associated with its illegal disposition. It was common knowledge among the police and FECB investigators that some miners stole high-grade ore, often putting it in condoms and inserting them in their rectums in order to escape detection as they left the mine. They then sold the gold ore locally to someone who had the means of refining it and disposing of it in the illicit gold trade. The illegal refiners were so skilled that they could often refine gold to the rate of "900 fine", very close to the "1,000 fine" that is the standard for pure gold.

The Ontario Provincial Police (OPP) had a completely inadequate high-grading squad, only one man working out of Timmins. He had informed the FECB group that he suspected that gold produced by the illegal refiners was being disposed of in the United States. If so, the FECB was losing the foreign exchange that should have been processed by the Bank of Canada, probably millions of dollars a year. Although the OPP was responsible for enforcing the Criminal Code, it had no particular interest in this federal matter of the illegal export of gold. Max Fell's group had a profound interest in it.

Inspector Schutz, Max Fell, and the Deputy Attorney General of Ontario, Bill Common, met to discuss the situation. As a result, Fell's group took over the investigation of certain high-grading activities of the group, which required more RCMP assistance than McElhone alone could give. Hence my transfer to the FECB investigative group.

Our interest in the case extended beyond local high-graders and refiners. Our main concern was to track down the people who later disposed of the gold, and who presumably arranged for it to be smuggled into the United States. This was no small task, considering all we had to go on in the beginning were suspicion, the knowledge that high-grading had occurred in years past, and the assumption that it had never stopped.

In addition to Fell, McElhone and me, our group contained Bill McKee, a short rotund Irishman who had formerly helped investigate high-grade cases when he worked for the Ontario Securities Commission. He thus had knowledge of the people involved at that time, and their modus operandi. His last case had centered on Simon Dollinger, still serving a five-year jail term in Kingston penitentiary.

McKee directed us to an obvious starting point – the public assay office of William Heys and Son. It was situated on the second floor of the Arcade on the east side of Yonge Street, about three blocks south of Queen Street. For a fee anyone could have gold assayed there. We began to keep watch on the Heys office in order to identify any visitors who took gold there for assay, but who apparently were not associated with any legal gold business. After every such visitor left, father and son cooperated with us by allowing us to examine their records.

We found many names of potential suspects, although we knew that the names they gave for Heys' records were false. They used to leave their gold samples, usually in the morning, and telephone for the assay results later in the day, so that they had no further contact with the assayer. This method, plus the false names, must have seemed to the high-graders to be a safe way of operating.

Even if the high-graders had recognized the Heys office as an Achilles heel, they had no other way of knowing the true value of their ill-gotten gold. In any case, it was not the responsibility of Heys and Son to ask customers about the source of their gold samples, or even to tell the police of their suspicions. But when Heys knew why we were checking their records, they allowed us to do so without any search warrants, knowing of course that we could always obtain warrants, although with some inconvenience. They also refrained from warning their customers that the police suspected them of illegal activities.

McKee's past experience had shown that those who smuggled gold into the United States received payment in U.S. money. Before returning to Canada they exchanged it for Canadian $1,000 bills. We knew it would be useful evidence if we could find some trace of such bills either in Canada or the United States.

We made inquiries at a number of Toronto banks. At one bank we learned that a father and son often exchanged Canadian $1,000 bills. The manager said he didn't know their names. We suspected that he knew but was disinclined to tell us. He did say, however, that the older man always carried a pair of pants over his arm. A tailor, perhaps?

The Heys office records showed that two of their earlier customers, a father and son, had used the name of "Wurtler", although neither had recently brought in any samples. According to the bank manager, though, they were still changing $1,000 bills occasionally. The younger Heys recalled two important facts: the elder "Wurtler" usually carried a pair of pants over his arm, and the young "Wurtler" had once mentioned that he was studying optometry at the University of Toronto.

Meanwhile, we checked a number of northern Ontario banks to see if any Canadian $1,000 bills had shown up there, which, if so, might give us a lead to the local high-graders. No luck! But an earlier FECB case, on which McElhone had worked, offered a lead. A Dutch woman immigrant had arrived in New Brunswick with a large amount of jewellery, and had sold it there. FECB investigators in that province learned that she was regularly sending $1,000 bills to a bank in Toronto. They notified the FECB group in Toronto of this and suggested that the circumstances might warrant looking into it. Inquiries at the Toronto bank revealed that the Dutch woman had sent the bills to the bank for safekeeping, and that she had retrieved them on periodic visits to Toronto.

On her next visit to Toronto, McElhone observed her boarding a train for Niagara Falls. He boarded the same train and questioned her as she went through Customs there. She produced a number of $1,000 Canadian bills, and admitted she had taken other $1,000 bills to New York City on earlier visits. There she had changed them into U.S. funds with a money broker whose name she gave McElhone, and then had deposited the money in her New York bank account. Later she was charged with illegally exporting money contrary to the FECB regulations, and was heavily fined.

Our inquiries in New York revealed that the money broker kept a record of Canadian $1,000 bills. He had sold twenty of them to people he had suspected of giving false names, and had recorded the numbers. With these numbers in our possession we checked the Toronto bank where the man with the pants over his arm had cashed $1,000 bills. We learned he had cashed ten of the bills the New York broker had recorded. We concluded that he was the older "Wurtler", who similarly carried pants over his arm when he went into the Heys office, and that his $1,000 bills were connected with gold smuggling into the United States.

Our next step was to try to discover who the two men calling themselves "Wurtler" really were. Remembering that "young Wurtler" had said he was studying optometry at the University of Toronto, we checked its records. We found that a young man by the name of Sydney Faibish fitted the Heys office description. We borrowed Faibish's class photograph, and Heys recognized him as "young Wurtler".

From the university records we had also learned that he lived with his family on Grace Street, off College Street in west-central Toronto. On checking into his background we were not surprised to find that the man with the pants over his arm was his father. We were surprised, though, to learn that Sydney was the nephew of the Simon Dollinger serving five years in Kingston penitentiary for high-grading offences. By this time, however, the Faibishes were no longer leaving samples at the Heys office, so we began to wonder if they were still in the "gold business".

Meanwhile we continued our observance of the Heys office. Over the next few weeks we saw a number of men separately visit the assay office several times with gold samples. All of them followed the same procedure of leaving samples in the morning and telephoning for the assay results later in the day. We investigators still believed that all of them gave false names to Heys. Moreover, the Heys records showed that assay results were uniformly high. Heys and his son agreed with us that the samples must have come from high-grade gold, and that the men came to Toronto from northern Ontario.

For some time we had followed every suspected man who left gold samples at the Heys office. We believed that each one had gold in his possession from which he had taken samples for assay, and that he would dispose of it when he received the assay results. In order to identify our suspects we needed their photographs, but we couldn't easily photograph them without giving ourselves away. Fortunately, several street photographers were operating on Yonge Street. We had them photograph each suspect as he emerged from the Arcade on Yonge Street. Later, we sent the photographs to the Timmins and Kirkland Lake police, who identified them and gave us their names. They all came from one of two groups, either the large Lebrecque family from Timmins, or a group of Italian Canadians from the same general area.

As we followed the suspects when they left the Heys office, each in turn led us to 14 Wells Hill Avenue, in an above-average residential area in the Bathurst Street-St. Clair Avenue district.

We then watched the house, noted the times at which the suspects arrived and left, and checked with the Hays office to learn the time each suspect telephoned for his assay results. About half an hour after receiving them they left the house and made their way back to northern Ontario. From the license numbers of the cars they drove, we found that the car owners were the same people as those identified for us by the police in the north.

We were not surprised to learn that the occupant of the 14 Wells Hill Avenue house was Annie Newman, who was well known to the police of southern Ontario. Annie, then 51 years old, had formerly been the paramour of Rocco Perri, Canada's Public Enemy No. 1, who had been interned when Italy declared war on the Allies in June 1940. Perri was involved in Mafia-like crime, and Annie was just the kind of woman to support him.

She had come from Poland to Canada in 1907. Before living with Perri she had been a well-known bootlegger in Toronto. Later she had worked with Perri as a bookmaker in Hamilton. We were especially interested to learn from police sources that Annie Newman had at one time been involved with Perri in the purchase of high-grade gold. Perri, it was alleged, had concealed a shipment of high-grade gold for a high-grader, had stolen it from him, and so became involved in the high-grade gold racket. Incidentally, when Perri was released from internment at the end of the war, he disappeared. Police sources claimed that his enemies had given him "a coat of cement" and had dropped him into Lake Ontario.

Annie Newman had never been convicted of any crime, even though the police strongly suspected her of being involved in Perri's criminal activities. Alphonse Labrecque, one of the high-graders, once said of her, "She has the pure white hair of a woman of 70, the face of a woman of 30, and the body of a girl of 16." A member of the RCMP added, "and the cold hazel eyes of a killer." If indeed she was the recipient of the gold, as we suspected, we now had to find out how Annie disposed of it and to whom.

Meanwhile we kept wondering why the father and son Faibish were no longer taking gold samples to the Heys office. Before long we learned that our two problems were linked.

As soon as we knew Annie was involved with the high-graders, McElhone and I used a vacant house, with the permission of the owner, as a base to watch Annie's house. Our lookout was so situated that from a second-storey, back-bedroom window we could see into her living room. Whenever she and a suspected high-grader did their calculations near the living room window, we saw exactly what they were doing. We were not entirely surprised to see a young man, who we were later to know as Sydney Faibish, arrive on foot at Annie's house, about thirty minutes after each high-grader left. He stayed there about an hour, then returned directly to his home on Grace Street. We now had a link between Annie and the probable purchaser of the gold.

After we knew the high-graders were meeting Annie at her home, we stopped watching the Heys office as we could check their visits to Heys from his records. Similarly, after Faibish came into the picture, we stopped watching Annie's house and concentrated our surveillance on the Faibish house. We hoped that surveillance would enable us to learn how the gold Faibish received from Annie left his possession, most likely en route to the United States, in view of Faibish's connection with Simon Dollinger.

Keeping surveillance of the Faibish home was no easy task. Grace Street was normally a busy residential thoroughfare where numerous children played and the traffic was consistently rather heavy. McElhone and I spent many days and nights on the street, usually parked in various cars and vans, waiting for something to lead us to discover how Faibish disposed of the high-grade gold we believed he was continually getting from Annie. As it was summertime he was not attending classes at the University. He seldom left his home, except to go to the Newman house. We were thankful that he always went on foot, which indicated he had no car, and made it easier for us to follow him.

Unfortunately for us, after a couple of weeks of surveillance of the Faibish house, and continuous checking at the Heys office, we had learned nothing new. We still knew only that our suspects consistently left gold samples for assay, that they always visited Annie afterwards, and that Sydney Faibish was always her next visitor. Nothing indicated how Sydney Faibish was disposing of the gold. We began to think we were on the wrong track.

SIX

During our two weeks surveillance of the Faibish home we had followed Sydney Faibish, first to Annie Newman's home and later to the Metro Theatre on College Street, each time men from the north took samples to the Heys office. This strengthened our belief that when Faibish returned home he was in possession of the gold the high-graders had sold to Annie Newman. We had begun to wonder if our surveillance of the Faibish residence would ever bring us closer to finding what Faibish was doing with this gold. It made us think that perhaps he was getting rid of the gold by means which we could not detect.

During the time we were watching Annie's house, a member of the Ontario Provincial Police at Timmins arrested two members of the Labrecque family who were already in our net. He found them in possession of unrefined gold ore. They were each given two months in jail. This disturbed the high-graders, Annie, and Faibish. During the following week no samples were delivered to the Heys office, so no high-graders visited Annie's home. When the high-graders began again to take samples to the Heys office, they met Annie at the Metro Theatre on College Street, owned by her lawyer nephew. Faibish paid his expected visit after the high-graders had left.

At this stage we did not know what arrangement there was between Annie and Faibish. We didn't know if Annie bought the gold and sold it to Faibish, or if she was a partner of his in the overall scheme.

Later, after we had raided the homes of Faibish, Annie, and the high-graders, we questioned the lawyer, thinking he must have known what was taking place when Annie met the high-graders and Faibish at his theatre. We believed that he did know, but he denied any knowledge and we could not prove otherwise. He admitted cashing a few $1,000 bills for his aunt.

Wartime censorship, then in effect, allowed us to come into possession of a letter to Annie Newman. It appeared to be an answer to a letter she had written. It contained a cryptic message about a man named Shelman, who seemed to us to be assaying gold smuggled from Canada into the United States. When we brought the U.S. Customs into the picture we passed this information to them. They checked the U.S. Mint, where all U.S. refiners of precious metals are registered. The nearest name to Shelman that they could find was Shulman, a man who had previously held a license when he worked for Kuschner and Pines, a large wholesale jewellery firm in New York City.

We could not find any link between Annie Newman and Shulman. But we were ready to believe that Annie was probably trying to find someone in the United States who would assay smuggled gold. Then she could avoid having to depend on the Heys office for assays, and perhaps avoid having to deal with Sydney Faibish. By eliminating Faibish she would make a greater profit, and feel safer if the assay work was done outside of Canada.

Another intercepted letter told Annie to meet a priest at Timmins, Ontario, and to "bring up 35 and we will settle here." McElhone "tailed" Annie when she went to Timmins by train one evening. The train arrived at Timmins in the middle of the night and McElhone saw Annie meet the priest on the platform. Soon, along came one of our suspects, Alphonse Labrecque, the most noted high-grader in northern Ontario. The priest left. Annie and Alphonse sat on the platform until an eastbound train came along. We never found out if the "35" mentioned in the letter referred to money, and if it did whether it went to the priest or Alphonse. When Annie boarded the train, McElhone, without a sleeper reservation, followed her and was given the sleeping berth above hers for the return trip to Toronto. Later we learned that she had met the priest to ask him if he would intercede with his long-time friend, the Minister of Justice, Ernest Lapointe, about Rocco Perri's possible release from internment. But we could only interpret her meeting with Alphonse as being related to their gold dealings.

When we had first discovered Annie's involvement with the northern high-graders, we began to follow her wherever she went, because we didn't know at that time that there was no need for her to take gold samples to the Heys office. Whenever she left her home at 14 Wells Hill Avenue, she always acted as though she had to lose someone following her. When she entered the Eaton's store at Yonge and Queen Streets she used the elevators. She always got off at one floor and then waited for the next elevator to take her up or down to the floor she wanted, a well known maneuver in "shaking a tail". On the other hand, Annie helped us by always wearing hats with feathers. So, although she was short, we could always follow her in crowds by watching the feathers.

We never saw her go to the Heys office, so we checked with Heys to learn if any women had ever left gold samples for assay. One had done so a considerable time before and had given the name of Johnson. Heys description of Johnson convinced us that Johnson was Annie Newman. One day McKee saw Annie's photograph in a photographer's window. He borrowed it and showed it to Heys and his son. Johnson was indeed Annie Newman.

During the period we were checking on Annie, one woman visited her. A check at the Heys office showed that a woman, giving the same false name as given by a male member of the Labrecque family, had left a sample for assay that morning. She stayed at Annie's until she telephoned for the assay results, and left soon afterwards. Then she went by streetcar to the bus depot at Dundas and Bay streets. She immediately went to a bank of telephones, each separated by a clear plastic divider. I slipped into the next space and heard her ask the operator to put her through to a number at Timmins. She told her listener, "Everything's O.K. I'm taking the next bus home." Later, we checked the telephone number she had called. We learned that she was the wife of the Labrecque who always used the false name she had given, whenever he left samples at the Heys office. Later, when it came time to prosecute those involved in the conspiracy, it was decided not to charge her with an offence. But she was included in the indictment as a co-conspirator, so that evidence of her involvement could be used to link her husband with her visit to the Heys office.

The unexpected arrest of the two Labrecques in Timmins proved useful to us later. When the O.P.P. constable searched their homes he found two small notebooks which contained dates and assay results which corresponded with those in the Heys office records. The notebooks also had the dates of their visits to Annie at home and at the theatre, and the later visits by Faibish to Annie at both places to pick up the gold. They also fitted the dates we had kept of such visits.

One Saturday afternoon, after we had been watching Faibish for a couple of weeks and feeling more pessimistic than usual, our surveillance paid off. An almost new blue Buick sedan pulled up to the Faibish house. Two middle-aged men got out and walked up to the house, waiting to be asked in. We drove past to check their car and were delighted to see it was an American car with a New York State license. When the men came out we noticed that one was bent over, as if burdened by a heavy weight under his jacket. He got into the passenger seat. When the two drove away we followed them. We expected them to go directly to the Queen Elizabeth Way, en route to Burlington, and then to Niagara Falls, Ontario or Fort Erie, Ontario, en route to either Niagara Falls, N.Y. or Buffalo, N.Y. To our surprise they stopped at the streetcar terminal restaurant on Queen Street at the western edge of the city. We followed them inside and saw them sitting at the counter. McElhone and I sat down beside them.

"Is that your good looking Buick out front?" I asked the man next to me. He nodded.

"My friend and I are breaking it in. We came over to Canada to put a few miles on it."

McElhone leaned over. "We're going to the States for a weekend," he said, "I hope our old Ford will get us there."

"We're going home to Buffalo," the overburdened man said. "If you're going our way you don't need to worry. We'll be traveling slow, so you can keep up with us. If you get into trouble, we'll help you."

"Thanks," I said. "Thanks a lot."

At that time the policy of the RCMP was to trade in police cars only after they had gone over 100,000 miles, and then only if absolutely necessary. Our unmarked car had gone many more miles than that. We were glad to hear that they would be "traveling slow", and that their destination was Buffalo, N.Y.

All the time we were talking I was aware that I sat next to the man carrying a load of gold that he had obtained from the home of the man we now considered the key operator of the Canadian ring of high-graders. It was hard not to arrest him and his companion. But McElhone and I had reluctantly decided that we should allow this load of gold to go through U.S. Customs, then report to U.S. Customs what was taking place. There would be other loads their investigators could follow to develop their own case, which could be eventually linked with ours.

When the two men left the restaurant, McElhone and I accompanied them to the cashier's desk and then outside to their car, which we duly admired. True to their word they traveled slowly, not necessarily to break in their car, we thought, but to make sure the police would not pick them up for speeding. In fact they went so slowly that we drove past them, waving as we went by. They waved back. Later, so as not to get too far ahead, we stopped on the side of the road, pretending that we had trouble with our car. They stopped to ask if they could help, but we explained that we had thought, wrongly, that our car was getting a little hot.

From that point we followed them through the Burlington cut-off, to make sure they were indeed headed for the United States. Then we felt free to drive back to Toronto. Before doing so, however, we stopped and telephoned Corporal Harry Allen at the RCMP Fort Erie detachment, asking him to watch for the blue Buick as it crossed into the United States. That evening he telephoned to say he had seen the car enter the United States at Buffalo.

On Monday morning Max Fell and Bill McKee flew to Washington. Because our case involved gold, they discussed the matter not only with the U.S. Customs, but also with the Secret Service, and gave them the information we had on the blue Buick and its occupants. After that the two U.S. enforcement agencies co-operated with us and each other.

About ten days later, the same two men we had followed arrived in the same Buick. Again they entered the Faibish home. When they came out, one man again walked as if carrying a heavy hidden load. Instead of following the car we telephoned the U.S. Customs at Buffalo. As we had agreed, they waited for the car at the Peace Bridge, then followed the two men to their homes, without making an attempt to seize the gold. That evening, a U.S. Customs investigator telephoned us to say that they had followed the two men as planned, and had found that their names were Charles Abrahams, the car driver, and Harry Julius, the passenger and gold carrier.

The time had come when we had all the evidence we needed to charge eleven men and two women with conspiring to export gold into the United States. We were now waiting only for the U.S. Customs to seize the next load of gold that Abrahams and Julius received from Faibish, to put our search and arrest plans into effect. The first shipment of gold we knew about had been smuggled into the United States on September 13, and the second on September 23. The third, smuggled in on the night of October 4, was seized by U.S. Customs. They notified us immediately and we put our pre-arranged plans into action. We sent word to the RCMP detachments at Timmins and Kirkland Lake to proceed with the searches of the homes of the high-graders, and to arrest them. In Toronto, with the help of members of the RCMP, we searched the homes of Annie Newman and Sydney Faibish, who had been known to the Heys office as the "young Wurtler".

McElhone and I went to Annie's place. As she opened the door that early Sunday morning, just wakened from her sleep, she was alert enough to say, "You didn't have to go to all this trouble. If you had phoned I would have come down."

No doubt she would have done so, after destroying all traces of her involvement with the high-graders and Faibish. As it was, we arrested her and searched her house. We did not find any gold, but did find ample evidence, by way of records in several notebooks. They detailed the fineness and weights of the gold she had bought, also, the price paid per ounce to the high-graders, and a higher price per ounce that she received from Faibish when she sold the gold to him. This told us what her business relations were with Faibish. There were no names of high-graders in her notes, but we were able to deduce from whom she had bought the high-grade gold by its fineness. A check with the Heys office told us which high-grader had brought in samples of that particular quality, and the date the sample was received. Knowing the date, we could supply, from our observations, the identity of the high-grader.

McElhone and I arrived at the Faibish home during the course of the search. It was even more productive than the search at Annie's. In addition to records of Faibish's dealings with Annie and the Americans, we found jeweler's scales, five buttons of gold weighing from several ounces to several pounds, and more than $8,000 in Canadian cash, all neatly secreted in the basement. Because it was Sunday the prisoners found it impossible to obtain bail, and had to wait until Monday morning to obtain their freedom.

Later that day we learned of the seizures in northern Ontario. Similar notes were found there, recording the dates, weights and fineness of gold sold to Annie Newman. Again the dates and fineness of the gold samples corresponded with the Heys records. Weigh scales and paraphernalia required to refine gold were found in the home of Alphonse Labrecque.

That Sunday night the U.S. Customs informed us that the car driver, Charles Abrahams, and gold carrier, Harry Julius, had told them that the smuggled gold eventually found its way to Kuschner and Pines, wholesale jewellers in New York City. Julius had said that he always turned the gold he had smuggled over to Jack Rubin and David Roth, who then disposed of it to the jewellery firm of Kuschner and Pines in New York City. Rubin, we were told, was appealing a seven-to-twenty-year sentence for being involved in a theft of stolen jewellery. We were pleased to hear that the U.S. Customs had found in Julius's possession, records, not only of his dealings with Rubin and Roth but also with Faibish. They would make them available to us for our trials. Abrahams, Rubin and Julius had agreed to come to Canada to give evidence against Faibish. These men, they told us, would be made available to us to use as witnesses if we thought their evidence would help our case. It would.

Their evidence would enable us to trace each button of gold, from which the samples assayed by the Heys office had been taken, from Northern Ontario to Annie Newman, to Faibish, to the smugglers, and finally to Kuschner and Pines, refiners, in New York City. Equally important, these records showed that all concerned had been smuggling gold for a much longer period than we had been investigating the case.

With this evidence, and that contained in the two notebooks seized when the two Labrecques were arrested, plus all the evidence we had collected before and during the searches, we had more than enough evidence to charge all involved in the conspiracy.

After McElhone and I had first seen the American car at the Faibish house, and one of the men left as if carrying a hidden heavy load, we had asked the Department of Justice in Ottawa to appoint special counsel to prepare for the prosecution. The department appointed Robert Fowler to prosecute and John J. Robinette to assist him. There was some discussion about this not being proper as Robinette was a more senior lawyer than Fowler. But Robinette had found the case to be so interesting that he was prepared to act as a lower-ranking counsel. They drew up the indictments and we drew up the warrants to search, which we held in abeyance until the appropriate time.

A question arose as to which was the best procedure with which to conduct the prosecution. The lawyers decided, and we agreed, that a preliminary hearing, with about a dozen accused, and a score of charges against them, would result in the defence dragging out the hearings interminably.

With this in mind, counsel applied to the Attorney General of Ontario to be allowed to proceed by way of a preferred indictment, thereby obviating the need for a preliminary hearing. The Attorney General gave his permission, no doubt on the basis that it was undesirable to have charges under wartime regulations, the FECB regulations, hung up in the courts by legal wrangling and defence machinations.

The indictment charged ten men and one woman with conspiring to aid or abet the export of gold from Canada, contrary to the Foreign Exchange Control Board Regulations. One Italian Canadian was not charged because he was suffering from cancer; nor was the wife of one of the Labrecques charged for her part in making one sale of gold to Annie Newman. She and several others were included in the indictment as co-conspirators, for the purpose of using their activities as evidence to link up those of the main conspirators.

Before our trial began, U.S. Customs informed us that five men had been charged in a Buffalo court for offences arising out of their gold-smuggling activities. They were Charles Abrahams, the car driver; Harry Julius, his passenger and gold carrier; Julius' brothers-in-law, David Roth and Jack Rubin who had carried gold from Buffalo to New York City; and Bernard Kuschner, the owner of Kuschner and Pines, wholesale and manufacturing jewellers in New York City.

SEVEN

Even without lengthy adjournments, the "gold" trials lasted five weeks. That was an unusual time in those days. Court officials said it was the longest they could remember. The choosing of the jury on the first morning was slow as the half-dozen lawyers representing the accused rejected, for no apparent reason, seventy-four of the eighty-five talesmen called to act as possible jurymen. The acceptance of only eleven by noon meant the need for one more. The judge, Mr. Justice Keiller McKay, ordered the Sheriff of York County to bring extra talesmen from the street. From the thirteen he hastily commandeered the twelfth juryman was chosen. After the clerk of the court read the long indictment, the lawyers entered pleas of not guilty for their clients. During the following five weeks, seventy-eight witnesses gave evidence for the Crown, and identified hundreds of exhibits.

Between the time of the arrests and the trial, McElhone and I had prepared a long brief for the prosecuting counsel. It was usually the job of counsel to do this, but as we were so familiar with all that had taken place, they decided that we were the most competent to do so. And of course it saved them a lot of work. At the trial the staff sergeant in charge of the RCMP Preventive service had the job of following the brief, so that all the evidence of each witness was brought out, and that appropriate exhibits were produced.

The trials began with the Heys, father and son, giving evidence from their records to show the dates they had assayed gold samples for the accused, the results, and the names the accused had given them. They described how the assay results had been regularly requested by telephone in the afternoon of the dates they had given, and how they had assayed a total of 471 gold samples, brought in by the accused over the period set out in the indictment. They also identified each accused by the false names they had given.

The police presented the notebooks and pieces of paper seized in the homes of the high-graders in northern Ontario, and in the homes of Sydney Faibish and Annie Newman. These records contained notations of the dates they bought and sold gold, the weights of gold buttons and, most important for our purpose, their recording of the fineness of the gold samples Heys had assayed, and the dates they had received them. Comparing these figures with those in the Heys records, we were able to trace shipments of gold from the high-graders in northern Ontario to Annie Newman, then to Faibish, and finally to the two men, Abrahams and Julius, who smuggled the gold into the United States.

It was the introduction of similar records, seized by the U.S. Customs investigators from Julius, that enabled us to follow each shipment of gold, not only to Buffalo, New York, but to its final resting place, the factory of the wholesale and manufacturing jewellers of Kuschner and Pines in New York City. This was something we could hardly have hoped to do when we began the investigation a few months earlier.

McElhone and I gave evidence about how we had followed the accused from the Heys office to the home of Annie Newman, and how we had found out their real names. We explained how we knew they were still at Annie's house when the calls were made in the afternoons to the Heys office, asking for assay results. Then we described Sydney Faibish's visits to Annie soon after each high-grader left her house, and how he returned each time directly to his home. Our evidence included how we saw Charles Abrahams and Harry Julius visit the Faibish home, our discussion with them at the bus terminal restaurant, and how we followed them and the load of gold partway to Buffalo. We also described the arrest by the O.P.P at Timmins of two of the Labrecque high-graders who were suspects of ours, for being in possession of high-grade gold ore. These arrests led to a change of the meeting place of the high-graders and Annie Newman from the Newman house at 14 Wells Hill Avenue to the Metro Theatre on College Street.

Handwriting experts gave evidence to show that the writing in the seized notebooks was that of the accused from whom they had been seized. We made charts to assist the jury to follow the gold shipments from northern Ontario to Annie and Faibish in Toronto, and then into the hands of the smugglers, Abrahams and Julius, and then into the hands of Roth and Rubin in Buffalo, who disposed of it to Kuschner and Pines in New York City.

As the U.S, Customs had promised, four of the men indicted in Buffalo came to Toronto and admitted their roles in dealing with the high-grade gold. Julius told how he had received the gold from Faibish and paid him in Canadian funds, mostly $1,000 bills. He had been receiving gold from him for a much longer period than that of our investigation. He interpreted the notes the U.S. Customs had seized. As the Canadians had done he had listed weights and assays of the gold he had purchased, and the amounts received when he sold the gold to David Roth and Jack Rubin. He explained why he had paid Faibish in Canadian funds. It was because Faibish had told him that cashing American money in Canada in wartime was likely to draw attention to their activities.

Jack Rubin, another of the indicted Americans, told the court how, in 1938 in Toronto, he had contacted Simon Dollinger, out on bail, having been charged with high-grading offences, to find out if he could be supplied with high-grade gold. Dollinger introduced Rubin to Sydney Faibish. It was agreed that Faibish should buy gold from the high-graders and that he would take it to New York. He did this for a time and was paid in U.S. funds. He changed it into Canadian funds, mostly $1,000 bills, before he left New York. When World War II started, Faibish decided to stop smuggling gold into the U.S. He might be suspected of doing something illegal if he crossed the border too often. Then Rubin arranged for Julius to transport it. Abrahams gave evidence to say that he accompanied Julius when he picked up gold from Faibish, but that he was only Julius' chauffeur, and had nothing to do with dealing in gold. David Roth corroborated Rubin's story.

It was interesting to learn from the Faibish and Newman note-books the amount Annie paid the northern Ontario men per ounce of gold, how much Faibish paid Annie, and how much he received from Julius. From these notebooks we showed the jury how much Annie and Faibish made as "middle men". The northern high-graders received a good price for their gold, in the vicinity of twenty-three to twenty-five dollars per ounce, based on 1000 fine. Although Annie and Faibish only received two to three dollars and three to four dollars per ounce respectively, they had made the most money by dealing with many high-graders, yet doing very little work.

Bank tellers gave evidence of cashing Canadian $1,000 bills for Faibish and his father. Annie's lawyer nephew gave evidence that he had cashed forty-four such bills for her, many more than he had admitted when we first questioned him. We never believed that he was unaware of his aunt's dealings with northern Ontario high-graders.

Day after day the Crown's evidence built up against the accused, and one could sense an air of despair among them. When it was time for defence evidence, only the humorous Alphonse Labrecque, the dean of northern Ontario high-graders, and probably the most active one, gave evidence on his own behalf. Jewellers weighing scales had been found in his house. When we had tested the weights we had found they were an ounce or so heavy. When the Crown counsel questioned Alphonse about this discrepancy, he merely said, amid great laughter in the court, "Oh, those are my buying weights." He did not deny that he bought gold ore from miners and other high-graders, or that his scales were used to weigh gold.

When cross-examined on the similarity of the figures in his notebooks and those in the notebooks of Annie Newman and Sydney Faibish, he thought about his answer for a moment or two. Then, with a benign smile, he said, "It's a miracle." More laughter in the court.

"Are you known as the king of the high-graders?" Crown counsel asked.

"Well, not the king, but next to it," he answered.

I could only wonder why he had given evidence at all. With the evidence we had gathered against him, his own evidence simply showed his guilt even more clearly. He had actually been a good witness for the prosecution.

By the time the trial ended, we were on friendly talking terms with all the accused except Annie Newman. She had remained aloof since the first day of the trial. She had been embarrassed when she entered the courtroom, dressed as a very dignified old lady. The other accused, who knew she always dressed very youthfully, made fun of her. The next day she wore her normal clothes.

She was also embarrassed when the RCMP handwriting expert testified regarding the notes found in her possession. When the judge asked if anyone wanted to cross-examine the expert witness, Colonel Dick Greer, who represented some of the other accused, said loudly, "There's no point to it, Mrs. Newman can't read anyway." Annie's face went pink. She leaned over and spoke heatedly to one of the other accused who was laughing.

After five weeks of hearings, and after counsel for both sides had addressed the jury, the judge began his five-and-a-half-hour address to the jury.

"Gentlemen," he said, "if anything, in this case we have too much evidence". McElhone and I were pleased to hear such remarks, even though we knew the evidence produced was overwhelming.

Then the judge described the legal meaning of conspiracy, and went over the evidence in detail. Finally, because the accused were French, Italian and Jewish Canadians, he told the jury that the law knew no racial discrimination, and that they should divest themselves of all prejudice.

Mr. Justice McKay clearly charged for a conviction of all the accused. When the jury had been out deliberating for sixty-nine hours, however, crown counsel and the rest of us feared that hang-ups in the jury room might free some of the accused. When at last they did return with their verdicts, we were disappointed. Although the evidence had shown clearly that they were all implicated in the conspiracy, five were found not guilty: Franciotti, Mazucca, elderly Faibish, and Albert and Paul Labrecque. The jury failed to agree on the guilt of Alphonse Labrecque, leaving the Crown to decide if he should be tried again, This was not done, although Alphonse had virtually confessed his guilt when he gave evidence on his own behalf.

Five conspirators were found guilty of conspiring to export gold from Canada, contrary to the FECB(wartime) regulations. The two main offenders, Sydney Faibish and Annie Newman, were sentenced respectively to four years in the penitentiary and a fine of $7,000, and to three years in the penitentiary and a fine of $5,000. Ernest Labrecque received two years in jail and a fine of $3,000. Lionel Labrecque received two years in jail, and Franck Delucca fifteen months.

In dismissing the jury, the judge thanked them for their services over such a long period. He made no comment on the fact that, in spite of the overwhelming evidence, they had seen fit to free some of the accused. In sentencing those found guilty, the judge said he was unable to comprehend such reprehensible crimes, particularly in time of war, when men were dying on the field of battle to protect our freedoms.

"How the love or lure of gold prompted you to take such a course with conditions as they are in the world today is hard to understand," he said.

We the police understood well. Annie Newman had been associated with criminals most of her adult life. The rest of them, as they had done for years, simply took advantage of the opportunity to make easy money. The fact that Canada was at war meant nothing to them.

Both Faibish and Annie Newman chose to serve extra jail terms instead of paying their fines. Faibish later returned to his optometry studies, no doubt supported by the money he had obtained through his illegal gold operations. He later established himself in business in Toronto. After her release from jail, Annie never again came to police attention.

Thus ended the most extensive foreign exchange case during World War II. But it was only partly successful. We of the FECB investigation group were disappointed that Alphonse Labrecque had not been convicted. The evidence found in his possession, coupled with his visits to the Heys office with gold samples, the records found in Annie Newman's possession, and his virtual confession in the witness box, formed ample evidence to convict him.

Later we learned that the rumors we had heard during the trial, about the jury being "fixed", had some foundation, not only concerning Alphonse, but also others who were found not guilty. Even without additional information, it was reasonable to believe this in the light of the overwhelming evidence against them.

"It was sometimes a real Donnybrook in the jury room," one of the jurors told McElhone and me after the case ended.

Two jurymen had simply refused to discuss the evidence against Alphonse Labrecque. One of them had proposed to find one of the accused guilty (later found not guilty) if the other jurymen would find Alphonse not guilty. This they refused to do. These two jurymen then simply refused to discuss Alphonse's case, which resulted in the lengthy period in the juryroom. Similar objections were made to finding Alphonse's two sons, Paul and Albert, guilty. They were eventually found not guilty. Our juryman informant told us that by the time they came out of the juryroom, most of the jury felt rather fortunate that even five out of the eleven accused had been found guilty.

We knew one of the jurymen who had been "fixed". He was a golf course architect, well-known in the city of Toronto, and now down on his luck. He had been one of the jurymen picked up on the street when the list of the first eighty-five talesmen had been exhausted. We considered investigating this tampering with the jury, but we were faced with the obvious difficulties of getting people to talk openly. We had no choice but to allow the matter to die.

Meanwhile, the five Americans indicted in Buffalo, N.Y., were charged with conspiracy and aiding in the smuggling of gold bullion into the United States estimated in excess of $1,000,000. They were tried in the U.S. Federal court.

Charles Abrahams, Harry Julius, David Roth and Jack Rubin entered pleas of guilty. The owner of the wholesale jewellery firm in New York City, however, Bernard Kuschner, entered a plea of not guilty. McElhone and I went to Buffalo to give evidence of the

Canadian operation. This included seeing Abrahams and Julius visit the Faibish home, and our contact with them when they were carrying high-grade gold. The U.S. Customs officials gave evidence about the investigation they had made as a result of receiving our original information, and their seizure of Canadian gold at the border. They also gave evidence that, when Abrahams and Julius were arrested, Julius had twenty-three pounds of gold, worth $11,000, on his body, hidden in a specially made cotton vest, and $10,000 U.S., in cash. It was information from the U.S. Customs that they had made this seizure that enabled us to activate our prearranged plans for searches and arrests in Ontario.

In Julius's jacket they found the telephone number of David Roth, his brother-in-law, who in turn was a brother-in-law of Jack Rubin, and who was connected with the jewellery firm of Kuschner and Pines. Investigation showed that Rubin and Roth had purchased $662,000 in Canadian funds from one New York money broker since the spring of 1939.

When the firm of Kuschner and Pines was investigated, a former employee, Irving Shulman, identified photographs of the gold seized from Julius as being similar in form to gold he had refined for his boss, Bernard Kuschner. The smooth-talking Kuschner denied any knowledge of illegal dealings. Coincidental with the arrest of Julius and Abrahams, Kuschner's records of his gold dealings had been destroyed when sulphuric acid "accidentally" spilled on them. Shulman, who had been cleared of any involvement, said that during his time at the refinery there had never been sufficient sulphuric acid around to destroy even a few sheets of paper.

But the other four had their own axes to grind. In addition to pleading guilty in Buffalo and giving evidence in Canada, Abrahams and Julius were trying to work off as much as possible the punishment they expected in the U.S. federal court. They had given the U.S. Customs the facts about their gold dealings in Canada and the U.S. This helped the U.S. Customs bring the case to a much more satisfactory conclusion than it would otherwise have done. Roth and Rubin, who had a direct connection with Kuschner, were equally helpful, and for the same reasons – to work off some of the expected punishment in the U.S. federal court. All four gave evidence at the Buffalo trial which deeply implicated Bernard Kuschner in the disposal of the Canadian gold through his refinery workshop. The evidence of Roth and Rubin showed that they had supplied Kuschner with $2,600,000 worth of illegal gold.

Roth and Rubin were also responsible for the U.S. Secret Service uncovering, in the southwestern United States, a ring of jewellery thieves, all of whom, it was alleged, had sold their loot to Kuschner. The Secret Service believed that Kuschner was probably the biggest fence of jewellery in the United States. Being a manufacturing jeweller he could easily dispose of such loot in his company's workshop.

Kuschner received a sentence of four years in jail and fine of $3,000 on the gold offences. But he still faced charges arising out of the stolen jewellery.

Because Abrahams acted only as Julius's driver, and had given evidence for the prosecution in both Canada and Buffalo, he was given the light sentence of six months in jail. Julius, as a result of his assistance to the prosecution in both countries, was given one year in jail. Roth received the lightest punishment, a suspended sentence of two years. This we believed resulted from his being the main witness against Kuschner in the gold trial, as he would also be in the charges laid against Kuschner in the jewellery matter. He also faced charges arising out of the jewellery thefts.

Julius received the relatively light punishment of eighteen months in jail. But he received the promise of the federal prosecutor that when his appeal was heard on his conviction for possessing stolen jewellery, with the sentence of from seven to twenty years, he would say a good word on Julius' behalf. This promise must have been kept, because Julius had his sentence reduced to three and half to seven years in Sing Sing.

By the end of the gold case I had to reconsider my ambition to be a professional singer. I still took three and sometimes four lessons a week, whenever I could squeeze in the time. But I was so busy with police work that I realized I could not possibly achieve my goal on a part-time basis, with no time to practice. The time had come to give up the idea altogether.

In November 1941, after the gold case ended and before the trial began, I was promoted to the rank of acting corporal, only a year after receiving the appointment as detective. This meant that my fifty cents a day extra pay as a detective constable would be raised to seventy-five cents, and my basic pay raised seventy-five cents a day, a total increase of one dollar a day. In addition, my living allowance was raised from $1.65 a day to $1.85, a raise in all of a munificent $1.20 per day.

Nevertheless, the additional money was very welcome to a young married man. Acting rank was held for one year. In accordance with RCMP policy, I held the acting rank for one year, as a form of probation, before becoming a confirmed corporal. I was pleased to receive this recognition after being in the division for only two years. The circumstances of my transfer from Saskatchewan to

Toronto, at my own request, to study vocal training in my spare time, had made me think that this, and my situation as a newcomer to the division, would hinder any promotion I might have had under more normal circumstances.

The conclusion of the gold case ended my sojourn with the FECB enforcement group. I left McElhone, Fell and McKee to continue with other, but less exciting, FECB cases, and returned to the CIB.

EIGHT

Another case investigated by RCMP and FECB investigators, involving the lure of gold and the hope of riches it might bring, took place in Vancouver just before the Toronto gold case started. The planning of the crimes that were to take place began in Australia. Leo Edward Morland was a metallurgist employed by a large Australian gold syndicate. In January 1940, it sent him to New Zealand as the metallurgist for one of their dredges operating there. Morland was in charge of the daily output of gold, so it was easy for him to steal some of the less than fully refined amalgam from the laboratory in which he worked.

He had made plans for his criminal activity before he left Australia. He shipped 11 wooden packing boxes from his home in Australia to New Zealand. He cleared customs in Australia, and received a certificate of examination showing that they contained only books and laboratory equipment. What the customs officials did not know was that the boxes had been fitted with secret compartments in the bottom of each.

Each day, at the dredging site in New Zealand, he stole a few ounces of gold amalgam. When he had acquired enough of it, he "borrowed" company mercury to allow him to fully refine the amalgam at night. Then he returned the mercury the next morning. He falsified the company books to hide his criminal behaviour.

In a few months he had refined 3,997 ounces of gold and melted it into small bars, each about the size of a chocolate bar. These fitted into the slightly larger secret compartments in the packing boxes. The compartments were hidden under a sheet of plywood covered with green felt. On close examination the green felt appeared to be the bottom of the boxes. After the gold had been put in place he re-filled the boxes with books and laboratory equipment, to match the certificate he had received from the Australian customs.

Knowing he would have difficulty in disposing of the gold in both Australia and New Zealand, after nine months he resigned his position, saying he was going to Canada to open up a metals assay office. With no suspicion of his criminal behaviour, the company gave him letters of recommendation. He sent his boxes and three wooden chests to Auckland, where they remained in the Customs shed pending his departure for Canada from that port.

Still planning carefully, he did not show up there until a short time before the ship was due to sail. This meant that he would have to hasten through Customs if the ship was to sail on time. His boxes passed through Customs after a cursory examination, and a check of the certificate he had obtained from the Australian Customs when he had left that country to work in New Zealand some months earlier. So Morland sailed for Canada on the *S.S. Awatea*.

A day after his arrival at Vancouver, by showing the Australian certificate of examination, he had no difficulty in getting release of his boxes after only a cursory inspection. He then rented a room in an old office building, ostensibly to set up his assay business. Soon he found buyers for some gold bars, one bar at a time. What he was actually doing was looking for a situation in which he could dispose of all the gold he had brought illegally into Canada. On his arrival he had declared that he had brought in $700 in Canadian funds. But as the RCMP found later, soon after arriving he had bought $5,000 worth of bonds, a car, and had toured British Columbia without disturbing his $700 bank account.

Morland came to RCMP attention when they learned that a Vancouver jeweller, Martin Jacoby, was using unaccounted for gold in the manufacture of gold rings. They did not know that it came from two bars of gold purchased from Morland, or that he allowed Morland the use of his workshop.

Morland had no intention of selling his gold bars one at a time. He wanted to dispose of the $120,000 worth of bars that he had smuggled into Canada in one or two bulk lots. In this Jacoby promised to assist him. He assured Morland that in Seattle, Washington, he could dispose of it in one fell swoop. By now, Morland had found that his gold, assaying 965 fine, was not up to the 999.5 fine that was required by the Americans who might become its purchasers. So, using Jacoby's workshop, he tried to refine his gold to this standard, with little success.

Jacoby had made a special trip to Seattle to find someone who would buy a large portion, if not all, of Morland's gold. He returned with a man who tentatively agreed to purchase $60,000 worth, even at 965 fine. This man then received samples of Morland's gold and returned to Seattle to check on its fineness. A day later he went back to Vancouver and made a deal to purchase fifty-seven bars, if Morland would deliver them to Seattle on February 11 (1941).

On February 10, Jacoby helped Morland secrete the bars in his car. The plan was for Jacoby to go by bus to Bellingham, just over the border in Washington State, and be picked up by Morland after he had passed through U.S. Customs. Their plan blew up when U.S. Customs seized Morland's car after searching it, as well as the fifty-seven bars of gold they had found. Morland was arrested and charged with smuggling, for which he received fourteen months in jail. The RCMP was notified of the seizure and Morland's arrest, and went to Morland's room in the Vancouver hotel where he lived. Although the RCMP never received direct information, later they came to believe that the American who made the deal with Morland for the gold was an undercover agent of an American enforcement agency.

Meanwhile, Jacoby became anxious when Morland did not turn up as arranged. He telephoned his Vancouver hotel, using the name of Martin. Receiving no answer, he asked the hotel clerk to tell Morland to call Mr. Martin at a certain Bellingham number. Not only did the clerk recognize Jacoby's voice, because of his previous calls to the hotel, the clerk also told the RCMP of "Martin's" call to Morland and that he knew "Martin" to be Jacoby. On further investigation the RCMP found a U.S. Customs officer who, when checking a Canadian bus entering the U.S. early on the day Morland was arrested, recognized Jacoby as one of the passengers.

The RCMP found no incriminating evidence in Morland's room. Then they searched his office, in which they found fifty-three gold bars, hidden in the false bottoms of the chests he had brought from New Zealand. As Morland was in a U.S. jail, nothing much could be done with him until he had served his jail term. So the RCMP concentrated on Jacoby. Searching his place of business, the Pacific Gold Smelting Company, they found $1200 worth of gold being refined.

Jacoby returned to Vancouver to find an investigator of the Foreign Exchange Control Board ready to question him under oath. He lied to the investigator about his dealing with Morland, and as a result he was charged with misleading an officer of the FECB, even though he eventually told the truth.

Jacoby's son was also involved with Morland and he, too, lied about his connection with him. He, also, was charged with misleading an officer of the FECB. In addition, both father and son were charged with conspiring to export goods from Canada, contrary to section 573 of the Criminal Code, as well as being charged, under the FECB regulations, with aiding and abetting the illegal export of gold.

Jacoby received a fine of $4,000 on the conspiracy charge; a suspended sentence for misleading an officer of the Foreign Exchange Control Board, and he was fined $250 on one of the other charges. The rest were withdrawn. Jacoby's son pleaded guilty to the charges against him. He was fined but not as heavily as his father. On the conspiracy charges against the Jacobys', Morland, from his cell in a Seattle jail, gave evidence before a commissioner from Canada. It was admitted as evidence when the Jacobys were tried in Vancouver.

Morland's troubles were far from over. When he was released from the American jail in April 1942, he was deported to Canada to face charges under the Criminal Code and the FECB regulations. He pleaded guilty to all charges and was sentenced to the time he had spent in custody in Canada. Undoubtedly this mild sentence was influenced by the fact that by now the New Zealand authorities had requested that Morland be held as a Fugitive Offender. They wanted him returned to that country to stand trial on the offences he had committed there. After a lengthy trial in New Zealand, in which evidence was given by a U.S. Customs agent and RCMP Constable Harry Maxted, Morland was sentenced to three years in the penitentiary.

Due to delays by way of adjournments and the time spent between the preliminary hearing and the trial, Constable Harry Maxted and the U.S. Customs agent spent four months away from their respective countries. They traveled both ways in American army planes, often close to areas where the U.S. and Japanese air forces were in combat.

This case and the Toronto gold case, with different casts of characters and different plots, show that, wherever gold is handled, there are those who think that they can make easy money, even though it means committing crimes to do so.

I think it is safe to say that, wherever raw gold is handled, there are those who plan how to steal some of it, if they are not stealing it already. High-grading in Canada's gold mines has been a practice since the first mines produced gold ore. Modern methods have been devised to catch those stealing gold ore wherever it is mined. But it would be naive for those responsible for protecting it to believe that some gold is not leaving their property illegally. I am sure that the producers of gold in all parts of the world, whether in the Soviet Union, Australia, New Zealand, Canada or wherever, have the same problems in this regard.

Morland, in his New Zealand prison cell, had plenty of time to appreciate where his planning went wrong.

NINE

Within a few weeks of my leaving the gold investigation, I had surprising new responsibilities. I became the corporal in charge of a two-man squad to deal with various offences arising from the wartime regulations relating to the rationing of certain consumer goods and abuses of the price ceiling regulations. Constable Barry Graham and I were not part of any branch. In effect we were a branch of our own. I reported directly to the Officer in charge of the Criminal Investigation Branch.

The beginning of 1942 was the time of the "phoney" war, so-called in Canada because although many Canadian servicemen were going to Europe, they had yet to be engaged in combat. Nazi bombers continued their raids on Britain, and the city of Coventry was nearly wiped out in one spectacular raid. German U boats intensified their attacks on Atlantic shipping, and Germany's land forces reached the gates of Leningrad.

By this time the Japanese had bombed Pearl Harbour, and the U.S.A. and Britain had declared war on Japan. Earlier, in 1941, the British navy had lost three battleships. *H.M.S. Ark Royal* was lost to the Germans, *H.M.S. Prince of Wales* and *H.M.S. Repulse* to the Japanese. The only bright spot of 1941 was that the British had begun to counter German moves in North America. In Canada, recruiting for the armed services went ahead at a fast pace. The RCAF had established flying schools in various parts of Canada, and they were busy training not only Canadians, but also British servicemen and volunteers from other countries.

Soon after the outbreak of war in 1939, the Canadian government had established a partial price control system on such things as rents, sugar, timber, steel and clothing. Later it became obvious that such partial controls were not particularly effective, so the government put a price ceiling on almost everything, including wages and salaries.

As price ceilings were not in effect in the United States, there was need for a system to protect importers from the adverse effects of Canadian price ceilings. The Commodity Prices Stabilization Corporation came into effect, to provide subsidies for those importers affected, so that prices of imported goods, raw materials, and articles manufactured from them would not exceed the ceiling price at the consumer level.

These were indeed radical moves, made necessary to prevent rampant inflation and to ensure a fair distribution of consumer goods. Although such a thing was new to Canada, fixing prices for goods and wages had been used by King Edward III of England in the fourteenth century, to ensure the fair distribution of goods and services after the death of so many workers due to the great plague.

In 1940, in order to administer the rationing regulations, the federal government established the Wartime Prices and Trade Board (WPTB), with broad powers to enforce the wartime regulations relating to matters of rationing and price ceilings. Another newly established board, the Wartime Industries Control Board (WICB) made its own regulations to control materials of importance in the war effort, such as oil, rubber, gasoline and metals. In the matter of enforcement, both sets of regulations came within the purview of regional directors of enforcement, all lawyers appointed by the federal government from its patronage lists. Administrators, mostly one-dollar-a-year men, were appointed by the WPTB to supervise the various categories of rationed consumer goods. Controllers (again dollar-a-year men) were appointed by the WICB to supervise the use of materials upon which the armed services had the first call, such as gasoline and motor vehicles, but which in a limited way, and controlled by rationing, were also needed by the public.

The Foreign Exchange Control Board, whose regulations had led to the gold investigation of 1941, provided systems to ensure that Canada received all the foreign exchange possible as a result of its dealing abroad. Thus it could pay for goods purchased from other countries. Especially needed were American dollars for goods purchased in the U.S.A. The FECB regulations provided for the radical procedure of allowing their investigators to question persons under oath, and provided for punishment where the answers misled them.

A major concern of the federal government was the rising inflation. The cost of living in Canada had risen eighteen per cent between September 1939 and October 1941, in spite of the partial price ceilings and other measures. It was in October 1941 that the government set price ceilings, retail and wholesale, on all consumer goods. The ceilings set were based on prices between September 15 and October 31, 1941. At the end of World War II, it was known that the cost of living in Canada rose only three per cent from October 31, 1941 until the end of the war. Incidentally, during World War I, without any price controls, the cost of living in Canada rose sixty-five per cent.

To enforce both the WPTB and the WICB regulations, the government hired hundreds of inspectors, mostly men and women whose jobs had become redundant due to wartime restrictions. Among other things they checked to see if price ceilings in the retail trade were being adhered to. If not they referred the matter to the Board's regional enforcement counsel, who considered what action should be taken against the offenders. In most cases they were merely warned.

In Toronto, Mr. Dalton Wells, a future Chief Justice of the Ontario Supreme Court, was the regional enforcement counsel. In Ottawa, Mr. Wishart Spence was the senior enforcement counsel for the whole of Canada. Later he became a member of the Supreme Court of Canada.

By the end of 1941, the Wartime Prices and Trade Board realized that civilian inspectors, although able to check on prices and warn offenders, lacked the experience to deal with investigations leading to prosecutions. The WPTB turned to the RCMP for assistance. It was about this time, soon after the end of the gold case mentioned earlier, that I returned to the Criminal Investigation Branch. Within weeks I was put in charge of black market activities, with Constable Graham as my assistant. We soon became known as the Black Market Squad.

The dictionary definition of "black market" was:

In wartime a clandestine market for the sale of essential goods whose distribution is regulated and which are not on free sale.

It was our job to find those involved in such clandestine activities. We soon found plenty of offenders.

The first request for assistance came from a WPTB inspector

who had found the main Robert Simpson's store in Toronto offering a briefcase for sale whose marked price was above the ceiling price. On checking, Constable Graham found that Simpson's markup of 137 per cent resulted in a selling price far above the one set by the WPTB for such articles. He also checked with Eaton's across the street, and found the identical briefcase selling at sixty-seven per cent over the wholesale price, but within the ceiling price set by the board.

Mr. Wells, still reluctant to prosecute before a warning had been given, suggested we should warn Simpson's to bring the price down to the price ceiling or we would prosecute the company. I pointed out to Mr. Wells that the board did not ask the RCMP for its assistance just to give warnings to offenders, and that his inspectors could do it, as they had in the past. Graham and the inspector warned Simpson's to lower its price, but Mr. Wells appreciated my views, and very few warning were given after that.

A week later Graham checked Simpson's and found that they had not lowered the price. He seized the briefcase and Mr. Wells authorized prosecution. The company, represented by counsel, pleaded guilty and was given a substantial fine. The size of the fine was not important. The publicity following the prosecution showed the public that, if one of the largest retail firms in Canada could be prosecuted for a price ceiling infraction, the government meant business.

In this case, as in all WPTB prosecutions during the war, the federal Department of Justice appointed special prosecutors. These were local lawyers on the Liberal government's patronage list. This did not mean they were any less competent, but the fact was that many had no previous experience in prosecuting criminal cases.

I soon learned that the WPTB regulations had wide powers. They gave enforcement counsel powers to authorize searches without warrant and to seize, at any time, evidence that indicated a wartime regulation was breached. They also permitted officials of the Board to interrogate persons under oath if necessary. However, to my knowledge this authority was never used.

All infractions of the Board's regulations, even conspiracy to commit such infractions, were summary conviction offences. Conspiracy charges within the Criminal Code could be laid only for indictable offences. The summary conviction provision within the regulations was to ensure that they would be disposed of expeditiously in a lower court, rather than have indictable offences that would be dealt with in a higher court, with all the possible resultant delays by way of such things as preliminary hearings, trial delays and appeals. Such delays would have a disastrous effect on enforcement, if certain convictions were appealed, and there were lengthy delays before decisions were announced, as was often the case.

There was a means of appeal, however. Decisions of a magistrate's court could be appealed in the ordinary way to the County Court, and in parts of western Canada to the District court. The appeal was heard by way of a trial *de novo*, a new trial. Normally there was no appeal from the decisions of this court, but the WPTB regulations provided for an appeal by the federal government, when it became necessary, to the Supreme Court of a province. Such an appeal would only be made when a decision of the County Court had a severely adverse effect on the enforcement of the wartime regulations.

A further provision in the regulations allowed the government to license all businesses in Canada. Thus, any business that committed a WPTB offence could not only be fined, but also have its business license canceled.

Graham and I soon began to get information about how businesses operated when they wanted to charge for goods over the price ceiling. They simply took the amount over the price ceiling "under the counter" and never recorded it in their normal books of account. We were to learn, however, that in many cases two books of account were kept: one for the proper prices and one for "under the counter" payments. In cases where receipts were given, they would only record amounts according to ceiling prices.

We realized that to prosecute such people we would have to work undercover, hiding our true identities when making what we referred to as test purchases. The method was not strange to me. When I had arrived in Toronto less than three years earlier, I had worked undercover for a few days, mostly on Jarvis Street, buying drugs from peddlers, under the watchful eyes of members of the RCMP drug squad. But my career soon ended. Word got back to the drug squad that I was suspected of being one of the "horsemen" because my complexion was too fresh for a drug user.

Our squad's second case came to us on a platter. Two Toronto city policemen found two youths with genuine loose gasoline ration coupons in their possession. It was an offence to have coupons in one's possession if they were not attached to a gasoline ration book. The city police turned the case over to us. We found that the coupons had been stolen from a service station, and were being sold for twenty-five cents a coupon. Both youths were charged with being in possession of loose coupons, and the magistrate sent them to jail for three months, a much harsher penalty than they would have received a year hence when such offences were more common and the sentences lighter.

This showed that it was not necessary to have a ration book to obtain gasoline. Most service station operators accepted loose coupons. Unless they were found in the act of receiving a loose coupon, there was no way in which they could be prosecuted. Yet the success or failure of the gasoline rationing regulations depended on the service station operators observing the law. They were supposed to supply gasoline only for ration coupons they personally tore from the ration book issued to the vehicles into which they put the gasoline. This provision was widely abused. But service stations were in business to make money, and operators were most reluctant to force a potential customer to another service station that might accept loose coupons. In no time at all there was a flourishing black market in gasoline ration coupons.

The loose genuine coupons came from several sources. In small amounts, car owners gave coupons from their ration books to friends and neighbours. Thieves broke into transport company offices and stole ration books issued for their fleets of trucks. Thieves also broke into offices that issued ration books in the various regions. Service station employees stole coupons the station had received for gasoline, and sold them to other service stations. Truck drivers, who delivered gasoline to service stations and collected coupons for deliveries, stole large numbers and sold them, mainly to service stations that found themselves short of coupons as a result of selling gasoline without coupons. There seemed to be no limit to the sources of black market coupons.

In 1942, the first full year of gasoline rationing, counterfeit coupons came on the market rather slowly about midsummer, but in a flood that fall. The government authorities tried to ensure that the 1943 ration coupons would be more difficult to counterfeit, and this they did progressively for the next two years. But it did not deter the counterfeiters, and their coupons increased equally in quality. In each of the years 1943, 1944 and 1945, counterfeit coupons were available on the black market nearly as soon as the ration books for those years were issued. Document examiners at the RCMP crime laboratory began to categorize the peculiarities of the counterfeit ration coupons. In this way they were able to estimate the number of different counterfeiters who were printing coupons. By the end of the war, they estimated that there were at least a dozen different counterfeiters operating throughout Canada. When the gasoline ration coupons first appeared, and for a year or so thereafter, they were of such poor quality that it didn't take an experienced policeman to prophesy that we would soon be faced with a black market in counterfeit coupons. I had had some experience in cases involving the counterfeiting of money. I knew that when persons with the ability to produce counterfeit money plates saw how easy it would be to produce plates for counterfeit ration coupons, they would hasten to take part in such profitable crime.

The counterfeit ration coupons for 1945, in book form similar to the genuine ration books, had been counterfeited so expertly that a layman would find it most difficult, if not impossible, to tell the difference between them and the genuine coupons. I felt relieved when, in the spring of 1945, soon after the new gasoline rationing year had begun, when the end of the war was imminent, gasoline rationing came to an end.

Another factor in canceling the gasoline rationing was the expert quality of the counterfeit ration coupons. The Oil Controller and his officials decided that it would be senseless to continue rationing when it wasn't really necessary, and so have millions of gallons of gasoline directed to the black market by way of that year's expertly manufactured counterfeit ration coupons.

*T*EN

One of the first things to be rationed in wartime Canada was gasoline. The rationing system was based on each licensed car being allowed the basic ration book, the lowest category being AA. Any higher category depended on the car owner's occupation, and its relation to the war effort. For example, a candy salesman was entitled only to category AA, while a cattle buyer was entitled to category E, the highest. Even so, any higher category could be lowered if the car's mileage did not warrant the full category, according to a person's occupation. In such a case, either a lower category was issued or a proportionate number of coupons were torn from the higher-category book at the time it was issued. An application for the gasoline ration book had to be submitted to an office of the Oil Controller. It required the applicant to answer questions such as name, address, occupation and the number of miles he proposed to travel. If the application was approved, an authorizer in the Oil Controller's office stamped it to indicate the appropriate category of ration book. Then the applicant took his approved application to a ration book issuing office, usually an office that issued car licenses, and obtained his ration book.

Many occupations in which the use of a car was a necessity were allowed only an AA category. Travelers for companies whose products were considered non-essential found themselves out of work because their AA category ration books did not allow them to travel as extensively as necessary. Such salesmen could not expect to be favoured with a high-category ration book. All they did was encourage wholesalers and retailers to sell their products at a time when the government aimed at keeping both travel and the purchase of unnecessary goods to a minimum. It was not surprising, then, that persons accustomed to driving thousands of miles a year and using all the gasoline they needed, felt badly about being so severely restricted. Many of them had no compunction about trying to obtain a higher ration category than the one to which they were legally entitled. When their attempts failed, many traveling salesmen turned to the black market.

Others who lost their jobs because of government restrictions included senior company officials. Many of these found employment with the federal government, administering the wartime regulations. Unfortunately, many of them failed to administer the regulations honestly.

At first, Constable Barry Graham and I were anxious about our ability to obtain information on the abuses of the gasoline rationing regulations. We needn't have worried. We soon received information from service station operators who complained about their opposition abusing the regulations. Some of these operators continued to be useful informants, although we believed that they themselves didn't always obey the law. Even so, their information was usually reliable. Soon they told us about persons who offered them loose coupons for gasoline, and about service stations that made a practice of selling gasoline for loose coupons, or for no coupons at all. Whenever we investigated and prosecuted such cases we were careful to protect our sources.

Occasionally an informant told us about a person known to have acquired a higher-category ration book than his occupation warranted.

Such information from one service station operator, early in 1942, led Graham and me to a highly fashionable fur store on Bloor Street. At our request the store owner produced his gasoline ration book. It was the second highest category, a D, although his occupation entitled him to an AA category. He told us how an Oil Controller's employee, William Glenesk, who had been his own fur salesman, came to the store and offered him a way of obtaining a higher-category ration book than the AA to which he was entitled.

He also told us that Glenesk insisted that he must first lend him some money, although the store owner knew this was Glenesk's way of being paid for the ration book he claimed he could get. This led to a bargaining session in which Glenesk pushed for a higher "loan" for a higher-category ration book. Eventually the two agreed on a "D" category book in exchange for a twenty-five dollar "loan". Glenesk immediately produced a blank application form he said he just happened to have with him.

The store owner filled out the application, except for two spaces that Glenesk asked him to leave blank, those concerning his occupation and his proposed mileage. Later, when Glenesk returned with the application duly stamped with a D category, the fur store owner found that his occupation and proposed mileage had been filled in, but falsified. Nevertheless, he presented the approved application at the issuing office and received his illegal ration book.

From the moment Graham and I entered his store, the owner knew that he was in deep trouble, and seemed anxious to help us in our investigation. He didn't know what offences he had committed but, as we pointed out, the most serious was bribing a government official. With a test purchase case in mind, I asked him if he would introduce me to Glenesk as a friend who wanted to obtain a higher gasoline ration category than the one to which he was legally entitled. He agreed to do so. No doubt he hoped that any assistance he gave the police would lessen the punishment he was bound to receive on the charges that were bound to be laid against him.

As it was important that the store owner should not have time to alert Glenesk of RCMP involvement, I asked him to telephone Glenesk and suggest that he meet the store owner and me immediately, at a selected place. In a few minutes a meeting was arranged. I accompanied the store owner to a restaurant within a block of the Oil Controller's Spadina Avenue office. Graham, who had traveled behind us by police car, entered soon after.

The store owner and I were sitting in a booth having a cup of coffee, and Graham was sitting in the next booth when Glenesk entered. He was slightly built, about fifty years of age and rather poorly dressed. The store owner introduced me as his friend, Joe Aubut, the false name I had suggested. He assured Glenesk that I could be trusted, and immediately left the restaurant. I knew he felt badly about what he was doing, but he felt obliged to do it, if only because it might lessen the consequences of his own involvement with Glenesk.

"I'm a candy salesmen," I told Glenesk. "I'll lose my job if I can't get enough gasoline to make my usual contact with customers, but as a candy salesmen I'll never get anything higher than an AA category."

"You're right," Glenesk agreed. "The Oil Controller's planning to put your kind of business off the road."

"I'd like a category E book if possible," I told him. "How much will it cost me?"

"I couldn't get you an E," he responded. "But for fifty dollars I could get you a D."

"I'll give you seventy-five dollars for an E," I offered. He thought over my offer for a couple of minutes.

"All right, leave it to me," he said, after again trying to persuade me to take a D category for fifty dollars.

He mentioned that he was taking some risk, but had "fixed up others". He didn't mention what I learned later, that as an authorizer all he had to do was stamp my application with the category the information in it called for. In any case he had come for a deal. Taking a blank application from his pocket, he asked me to do what he had asked the fur store owner – to fill it out but leave blank the spaces calling for my occupation and intended mileage.

"I'll complete it and have the ration book approved by late afternoon," he said.

We agreed to meet again at 5:30 p.m. at the same place. He left the restaurant and a few minutes later I left, followed by Graham, who had heard most of what had been said. Before meeting Glenesk as planned, I arranged for Graham and another member of the now enlarged black market squad to observe us. I had already got them to record the numbers of the bills I would use to pay the seventy-five dollars to Glenesk. After the transaction in the restaurant, I would leave with Glenesk. As soon as we got outside, Graham and his partner would arrest him and retrieve the seventy-five dollars as evidence.

When I met Glenesk he gave me the application, duly stamped and approved for a category E ration book. I paid him the seventy-five dollars and we left the restaurant together. As prearranged, Graham and his partner arrested Glenesk, searched him and retrieved the money. Before Graham took him to the city police cell to await his appearance before a magistrate the following morning, I took him to our office to obtain a written statement from him.

"I knew it was a frame-up all the time," he commented before giving the statement.

By this time I had checked the completed application, and had seen that Glenesk had entered "cattle drover" as my occupation, and a proposed mileage of 40,000 miles for that year, enough for him to authorize a category E ration book. If I had really been a candy salesman, all I would have had to do would have been to present the approved application at an issuing office. No doubt Glenesk would have made the illegal procedure just as easy for many more future "customers".

The Glenesk case, the first of its kind, was a serious one, so the government appointed Mr. J.C. McRuer, K.C., later a Chief Justice of the Supreme Court of Ontario, as prosecutor. Even before his appointment as a judge he had the reputation of "being more of a judge than the judge".

McRuer, a tall, thin, austere-looking man with a manner to match, and a thin nasal voice, was considered one of Canada's foremost lawyers, and was often called on by the federal government for legal advice. We had had a few cases where magistrates had dismissed charges under the Wartime Prices and Trade Board regulations. When the government decided to appeal, Mr. McRuer was appointed in place of the original prosecutors who had dealt with the charges. He could now have authorized charges against Glenesk under the WPTB regulations, but instead he authorized me to lay charges of breach of trust under the Criminal Code.

At Glenesk's first appearance in magistrate's court he was released on $5,000 bail. At his preliminary hearing he was committed for trial in a higher court. Later he chose to be tried by a judge and jury in the Supreme Court. When he appeared there he pleaded not guilty.

He was so blatantly guilty that I wondered why his counsel had not advised him to plead guilty before a magistrate in a lower court. In that case he would probably have received less punishment than he was likely to receive in a higher court.

Meanwhile, we had enlarged the scope of the investigation. Various members of the black market squad visited a number of fur store owners and other persons related to the fur business. They had found many of them with ration books of higher categories than those to which they were entitled. In a number of cases some of the application forms had been falsified by Glenesk in the same way as the one he had processed for me, although others had been falsified by the applicants. Appropriate charges were laid against all offenders, and they entered pleas of guilty. Most went to jail for one to three months, and some were also fined.

At Glenesk's trial, these other instances in which he had received money for approving improper ration book applications led to his being faced with several more charges. Constable Graham and I, along with several of the offending store owners, gave evidence against him. So did an RCMP handwriting expert, who testified that on each application entered as an exhibit, Glenesk had written in the answers to the two vital questions about occupation and mileage.

When defence counsel cross-examined me, and again in his address to the jury, he stressed that I had tricked Glenesk by lying about my occupation and by using a false name. His defence was that on these grounds his client should not be convicted. He produced no defence witnesses.

Mr. McRuer, however, raised a more appropriate point. "This case is of far greater importance than it may appear at first blush," he said. "It strikes at the very vitals of good government."

He then rebutted defence counsel's charge that I had been dishonest. "When one goes out to catch a crook," he contended, "one has to be smart enough to catch him. Detective Corporal Kelly has brought to an end an iniquitous practice."

Mr. Justice Hope's charge to the jury was brief, but long enough to show that he thought Glenesk should be convicted on all charges. He pointed out to the jury that my use of a false name and occupation was quite proper. After about an hour's deliberation the jury brought in a verdict of guilty on all charges.

The judge adjourned the case for a week to consider punishment. During that week I learned from Mr. McRuer that Mr. Justice Hope wanted to sentence Glenesk to four years in the penitentiary. But Mr. McRuer insisted that two years less a day was sufficient. Finally, not altogether willingly, Mr. Justice Hope agreed to the lighter sentence.

When the case was resumed in court, defence counsel spoke to sentence by saying that Glenesk was a heavy drinker, and this was the reason he had resorted to the practice for which he had been convicted. I was amused, as usual, at this common practice of defence counsel. That is, although defence counsel knew his client was guilty, throughout a trial he steadfastly declared he was innocent. But after he was convicted, counsel would try to get as light a sentence as possible by explaining to the judge why his unfortunate client had been driven to commit the crime.

Mr. McRuer, knowing what the punishment was going to be, did not speak.

In passing the lighter sentence, however, the judge indicated why he was in favour of harsher punishment. He pointed out that the accused occupied a position of trust, even though a minor one. No government could carry on in these days of stress if men on whom it relied were lacking in integrity.

"I have to consider not only your position but the public generally," he declared. "The public are making sacrifices and should not be victimized."

This was not the first of many similar lectures I had heard magistrates give to accused convicted under wartime regulations, and I was to hear many more before the war ended.

Glenesk was only the first of a number of persons employed in Canada's rationing system to be convicted of breach of trust. But rationing was a national operation, and there were innumerable temporary employees with opportunities to use it to make easy money. It was safe to assume that an overwhelming number of abuses were taking place all over Canada, that were not coming to the attention of the RCMP. Indeed, during the following three years we heard that a considerable number of employees had been dismissed for improper behaviour. I am convinced that if these cases had been turned over to the RCMP for investigation, black market investigators across the country would have gathered sufficient evidence to warrant prosecution of most of those employees, and of those with whom they were illegally involved.

By the time the Glenesk case ended in May 1942, the Toronto black market squad had been enlarged to about ten men. Even then we had only enough men to scratch the surface of the many forms of black market activity.

Soon after the Glenesk case we had another case of a public servant abusing the trust placed in him. The Machine Tools Controller in Ottawa requested an investigation into the activities of Byron Dewy Snell, an American employed in his department. Snell was alleged to have received a bribe, for which he would favour a machine tools dealer whose business was located on Front Street at the foot of University Avenue in Toronto. It was alleged that, as a result of the bribe, the dealer expected to receive special treatment in obtaining machine tools from the limited supply available for public use.

When bribery involves cash paid by one person to another without records being kept, it is often impossible to prove it. In this case the machine tools dealer's account books did not reveal anything improper. But among the company's papers I found a note that, although not very clear, seemed to indicate that the dealer had recently disposed of a yacht valued at $3,000.

Further investigation revealed the yacht to be in the possession of Snell. There was no evidence to show that Snell had purchased the yacht, but we found a person to whom he had admitted that he owned it. The federal government appointed Mr. John J. Robinette as special prosecutor. He was at that time an advisor to the RCMP on legal matters, and he later became one of the best-known lawyers in Canada.

I laid a charge under Section 158(h) of the Criminal Code to the effect that Snell had received a commission, to wit: a yacht, without the permission of the head of his department. The offence came under "Frauds upon the Government" in the Criminal Code.

By this time Snell had left the employ of the government and was living in Vancouver, so it became necessary for the RCMP there to arrest him. When I flew to Vancouver to escort him back to Toronto, it was the second time I had been permitted to fly on police business. I flew from Toronto on a Trans-Canada Airlines Lockheed 14. It was one of the earliest planes used in Canada for transcontinental flights and, as its name implied, it carried fourteen passengers, seven on each side of the aisle. We stopped at Kapuskasing to refuel, in a thunder storm. When we stopped again at Lethbridge we changed to a "big plane" with oxygen, a twenty-one-seater D.C. 3 that would take us over the Rockies.

Compared with present-day flights, of 350-passenger planes at 500 miles an hour, my flight from Toronto to Vancouver in 1942 was a pioneering adventure. My twenty-hour flight meant leaving Toronto after dark one night, and arriving in Vancouver after dark the next. It also meant that, because of flight regulations, I was not able to carry a firearm on the return journey with Snell, as a member of the RCMP was expected to do when escorting a prisoner, even when in civilian clothes as I was.

Soon after I took Snell back to Toronto, he was tried as he had chosen, before a judge and jury. He pleaded not guilty.

Proceedings at the trial, however, indicated he was guilty. The machine tools dealer declared that he had given Snell the yacht in order to obtain preferred treatment in acquiring machine tools which were in short supply. Other evidence proved that he had taken possession of the yacht and had paid nothing for it. No evidence was produced for the defence, and when the judge addressed the jury it was obvious from his remarks that he favoured Snell's conviction.

After several hours of deliberation, however, the jury reported to the judge that there was no hope it could reach a verdict either of guilty or not guilty. My earlier experience in the gold conspiracy trials made me wonder if someone had tampered with at least one member of the present jury.

The judge dismissed the jury. He set the date for the new trial six months hence, and allowed Snell his freedom on $6,000 cash bail.

When the second trial was due to begin, Snell failed to appear, so his bail was forfeited. His counsel told the court that Snell had gone to the United States, and that as an American he had no difficulty in doing so. He had obtained a job with Henry Kaiser, well known then in Canada and the United States for the speedy building of 10,000-ton freighters, built to replace freighters sunk in the Atlantic by Hitler's submarines. The federal government decided not to apply for Snell's extradition from the U.S., and not to prosecute the machine tools dealer on whom we had depended to give evidence against him.

Snell was punished to the extent of the $6,000 cash that he had put up for bail, which was now forfeited to the Crown. But the offence he had committed warranted a term of imprisonment. One thing was becoming quite clear to the black market investigators – where there were offences under the war regulations, often there was corruption, punishable under the Criminal Code of Canada, among those responsible for their administration. By the time the war ended we had ample proof of this.

The Glenesk case showed us how widespread were the opportunities for corruption within the government offices dealing with rationing of the various commodities. We were soon to find out what little respect members of the public had for the rationing laws.

Gasoline rationing had been in effect only a short time when the St. Catharines police brought to our attention an incident in which they found a person in possession of a number of loose gasoline ration coupons. The law required that coupons remain in the ration books until they were removed by the gasoline supplier. Not being familiar with the new law, they wanted the RCMP to take over the case. I suspected that there was an additional reason. They didn't want to be involved any more than was necessary because of the prominent citizens who were implicated.

I went to St. Catharines and interviewed the person from whom the police had seized the loose coupons. He told me that he was an employee of McKinnon Industries, a subsidiary of General Motors of Oshawa. He had the job of attending to the heating systems in the homes of a number of high-level officials of McKinnon Industries. He visited each home once or twice in the middle of the night to ensure the furnaces were functioning properly. The homes included that of the general manager of General Motors in Oshawa, who lived in St. Catharines.

Because he used his car to make the visits to their homes, each official had torn coupons from his own ration book, and had given them to him so that he wouldn't have to use his own ration coupons for work he did for them. This would be a fair arrangement except that it was against the law in a number of ways. One was the tearing of coupons from the ration books, another was giving them to a person not entitled to them. The person found in possession of loose coupons was committing an offence, and he would commit another offence when he went to purchase gasoline for his car. This involved the service station operator, who should not dispense gasoline without tearing a coupon from the ration book of his customer.

I interviewed all concerned, who admitted what they had done. It had become known in the city that they had done something wrong, and that the police were investigating. To be found breaking a wartime regulation caused them great embarrassment. It was particularly so in the case of the general manager of General Motors.

I visited him in his Oshawa office. His staid female secretary told me that he was in a very important meeting and had asked not to be disturbed. I identified myself and told her that although I had not made an appointment to see him, I did not think that my visit would be unexpected. Without saying a word, she went into his office and returned with the general manager. He admitted that he had given some ration coupons to the man who cared for his furnace, not thinking he was doing anything wrong. He wondered if he would be charged and I said that I thought so. I took a short written statement from him and he went back to his meeting.

Charges were eventually laid against all concerned, and not one turned up at the hearing before Magistrate Campbell. Through their counsel they entered a plea of not guilty. The St. Catharines constable who had found the loose coupons and I presented evidence about the admissions of each person involved. The elderly magistrate appeared to be doing the job of defence counsel, and from the beginning seemed annoyed that the charges had been laid. In the end he dismissed all the charges on the grounds that he could not see from the way the law was written that the accused persons had committed any offence at all. The prosecution's case was not helped by the appointment of a junior and inexperienced counsel to handle the prosecution.

On my return to Toronto I recommended that the decision be appealed. At this stage of rationing it was important that the law be upheld, but if there was a flaw in it, that it should be amended as soon as possible. The Wartime Prices and Trade Board appointed Mr. J.C. McRuer, K.C. to conduct the appeal. At that stage and later, Mr. McRuer was only appointed to prosecute wartime cases when there was some difficulty in law, or if a case was more than usually important. The appeal was heard before Judge Schwenger of Hamilton, and as the appeal was based solely on the wording of the law, there was no need for witnesses. Judge Schwenger found all the accused guilty, and imposed appropriate fines. Nevertheless, the wording of the law was amended so that it was more easily understood.

Later, I wondered how the man who cared for the accuseds' furnaces got along without the use of loose coupons. I had no doubt that he continued with his job.

ELEVEN

Administrators appointed by the Wartime Prices and Trade Board (WPTB) worked under the authority of the Wartime Prices and Trade Board regulations. Each generally supervised the distribution of goods and services of direct concern to the consumer, such as foodstuffs and prices. Controllers, on the other hand, were appointed by the Wartime Industries Control Board (WICB) to supervise the use and distribution of particular materials of vital concern to the war effort, including gasoline, rubber and metals, which also were used by consumers. The WICB had its own general regulations, which authorized it to enact other regulations covering the restrictions placed on each of the materials for which the WICB was responsible. For example, in the case of gasoline, the Oil Controller had established his own regulations.

The Metals Controller also had his own regulations. He was responsible for all metals used in the war effort, but it was his interest in the scarce metal, cadium, that led him to request the black market squad to investigate a suspected abuse in the use of that metal. He had received information that a metal plating company in west Toronto was using more cadium than its output warranted. He informed us that cadium was so scarce that its use was limited to the plating of certain parts of radios used in fighter and bomber planes.

Our inquiries and observations led us to believe that the plant employees were stealing one-and-a-half-pound balls of cadium, and disposing of them through a men's wear store on Dundas Street

West. In studying the metals regulations I had found that they provided no offence for mere possession, but only for selling the metal illegally. Nevertheless, there was always the Criminal Code to fall back on. The buyer could be charged with receiving stolen goods, although charges under the wartime regulations were preferable.

It was important to put a stop to the drain on the plant's cadium supplies as soon as possible, and it seemed like a waste of time to investigate each employee who might be involved in the theft. Not knowing where the men's store owner might be keeping the stolen cadium, I visited the store one Saturday afternoon, posing as the owner of a plating company in Montreal. I gave the owner a long story about the shortage of cadium. The amount allowed by the Metals Controller did not permit me to use it for anything but the plating on military plane radios, for which I had a government contract. However, I had other projects requiring cadium plating, and I was prepared to purchase all the cadium he had.

I knew exactly the price of cadium, and offered him double. When he hesitated, I suggested that if he would not sell me his cadium perhaps I could make a deal with his suppliers. He refused to reveal them, or the price he paid them for the cadium. When I raised my offer by twenty-five per cent, he agreed to deal with me. I could afford to be generous. I had no intention of allowing him to keep whatever money I paid him.

He took me down to the basement of the store and showed me several cardboard cartons full of small one-and-half-pound balls of cadium. He had 400 balls, weighing about 600 pounds in total. He wanted me to take them away immediately, but I said I had come unprepared, and would have to ship the metal by rail to Montreal. As this was a Saturday afternoon, I explained, the rail offices were closed so I couldn't ship the metal until Monday. He agreed to spend all day Sunday making wooden boxes, and to deliver the metal in them, ready for shipping, on Monday morning at the CPR freight yard on Front Street. I paid him some money on account, using marked bills, and promised to pay the balance when he delivered the cadium at the CPR siding.

On Monday morning he arrived in a small truck, complaining about having spent the weekend making boxes and packing the metal. I helped him unload and then finished paying him the amount agreed upon, also with marked money. As he was about to drive away, two members of the black market squad arrived. They had been watching the proceedings, and had kept a record of the marked money I had used, not only then but also on the previous Saturday. They arrested and searched him. They retrieved the marked money I had just paid him, but also that I had paid him on Saturday afternoon.

He was charged under the Metal Controller's regulations. He pleaded guilty and was heavily fined. I turned over what information we had about the theft of the metal from the plant to the city police, so that they could deal with the Criminal Code charges if they wished. But I didn't hear from them again, presumably because they had decided the matter had been dealt with sufficiently by us.

By this time the members of the black market squad regularly investigated infractions of the gasoline rationing regulations. Their investigations took them to various war industries. They found that traffickers in gasoline ration coupons were usually employees of these industries, who thus had many potential customers among their fellow employees. Invariably a number of prosecutions resulted at each plant.

On a visit to a plant in Weston, on the outskirts of Toronto, Graham searched a suspect's locker, in which he kept the clothes he wore at the plant. Graham found a number of eight-coupon sheets of genuine coupons. The lithographing company, Rolph, Clark Stone held the sole government contract for the printing of gasoline ration coupons. The coupons never left the plant legally until after they had been made up into ration books with four coupons on each page. Graham knew that the sheets he had found had been stolen from the plant. Moreover, he could see that the eight-coupon sheets had been roughly cut from the larger sheets that the company printed.

Recently one of the officials responsible for supervising the printing had told us he suspected that sheets of coupons, containing 280 coupons each, were being diverted from the plant without going into the ration-book-making system. He had no idea who was responsible. But he had run a test, and had discovered that the number of sheets printed did not correspond with the made-up ration books. There were fewer books than expected.

Graham's questioning of the man from whose locker the coupons had been seized led him to a former employee of Rolph, Clark Stone. "Duke" Marshall had been fired for misbehaviour, but was still in contact with some of the employees. Graham's further inquiries led to four plant employees with whom Marshall was friendly. They in turn were friendly with two employees who operated the multicolour presses that produced the gasoline ration coupons.

During a lengthy investigation, searches of the homes of the suspects produced evidence of their involvement. Marshall and six employees, including the two pressmen, were charged under the Criminal Code with theft. All were convicted. The ringleader, Marshall, received two years in jail, and the others were heavily fined. An extended investigation by the other members of the black market squad, of those who had become a part of Marshall's gasoline ration coupon ring of traffickers, resulted in other convictions. In addition, a number of people were convicted who had purchased gasoline ration coupons from them for their own use. Four of the six Rolph, Clark Stone employees were fired. The two pressmen were retained because they could not be replaced.

This case was an example of the many cases we handled. There was no such thing as only one person being involved in an offence against the many rationing regulations. For each person in possession of loose ration coupons, there must have been a supplier. And the possessor of the loose coupons could only use them if a third person accepted them. Furthermore, each person involved was committing an offence against the rationing regulations.

Soon after the above case, Graham and his partners investigated a case involving a twenty-five-year-old woman. She was an employee of the Oil Controller in the office on Spadina Avenue – the same office in which William Glenesk had been employed when we arrested him for selling high ration book categories for seventy-five dollars. It was this woman's job to issue ration books on the basis of the time left in the rationing year. For example, if six months had gone by, she would tear out half the coupons from whatever category book to which the applicant was entitled. She was supposed to put the loose coupons in a safe container, so that periodically they could be sent to the firm of Hinde and Dauche's waste-paper plant for destruction. Instead she placed only some of them in the container, and some in a place where she could retrieve them at the end of the day's work.

This investigation began when a service station operator who had been turned down for active service, and who regularly gave us information, told us that the owner of a certain car, whose license number he had taken, had offered him loose genuine coupons for gasoline. He had dispensed the gasoline, and had taken the loose coupons as we had advised him to do. Thus when we checked the car's owner, he would not think that the service station operator was responsible for it.

The owner and driver of the car was a nationally known orchestra leader. For some years he had led an orchestra that broadcast over national radio from the Royal York hotel. He admitted to us that he had obtained loose pages of coupons from a friend who, he understood, had received them from someone else. When interviewed, his friend admitted that he had received them "for a price" from a woman employee of the Oil Controller's office. He had approached her when a friend of his had advised him he could get coupons from her. Graham obtained the name of his friend, who told him the name of the woman employee. Each person interviewed produced the coupons he had obtained illegally, and all were eventually prosecuted.

Graham telephoned the employee, and told her that he had been speaking to a person to whom she had sold some coupons. Giving her this person's name, he said he would like to get some also. The necessary arrangements were made and the sale took place. As a result she was arrested, charged with breach of trust under the Criminal Code, and sentenced to nine months in jail.

By this time the black market squad had been permanently enlarged to ten men, in order to deal with the increase in offences under various regulations. Even with this increase in manpower, we knew that we were still only scratching the surface.

Some time after the woman ex-employee of the Oil Controller's office had been released from jail, I met her on Yonge Street. She told me she held no grudge against the police, not even Constable Graham, the investigator on her case.

"Constable Graham is a very nice fellow," she said.

By the time the war was three years old there was more and stricter rationing of foodstuffs, mostly meat, sugar and butter. An informant came to my home late one night and presented me with several large uncut sheets of genuine sugar ration coupons. Each contained hundreds of coupons. He had obtained them from a pressman at Consolidated Press on Adelaide Street, the company that printed Saturday Night magazine, and had a contract for printing such coupons. He had given the pressman a bottle of Scotch. My informant believed that not only he, but also many others had received coupons from the pressman.

The more I spoke to the informant about his meeting with the pressman, the more I became convinced that if he had not given him the bottle of Scotch, it was doubtful if the pressman would have given him the coupons. It had the elements of creating an offence when none was intended. But rather than leave the matter at that point, I decided to interview the pressman.

I went to his apartment on Sherbourne Street one Friday evening. At least, I thought, my visit would put a stop to his taking coupons from the plant. He denied doing so at any time, and to protect my informant I did not mention his name. But I was sure that the pressman was the source of the sheet coupons now in my possession. When I noticed on a mantel a picture of a young man in navy uniform, I told the pressman he should be ashamed of himself. His behaviour was indirectly creating a danger for our sailors who convoyed merchant ships from sugar-growing countries in the Caribbean. For all I knew, I said, they were being torpedoed at that moment.

On Monday morning the city police called me to ask if I would go to the city morgue to see if I could identify the body of a person they had taken out of the lake on Sunday evening. I identified him as the man I had interviewed on Friday evening. The police said they knew he had worked for Consolidated Press, and that he had a son in the navy who had been declared missing a week before. I did not ask the city police why they thought I might be able to identify the body of the drowned man. I later realized they had interviewed someone at Consolidated Press, and as I had spoken to Miss Sutton, the head of the company, before I interviewed the pressman, they learned that I had been in touch with him recently.

One feature of black market activities was that otherwise ordinary, law-abiding citizens gave little thought to the far-reaching consequences of their disregard of the rationing regulations. Perhaps they thought that what they were doing as individuals had little effect on the rationing system. But when such activity was multiplied by millions, the effects were serious. It was not as if they were not warned sufficiently. Rationing convictions were widely reported in the news media. Magistrates and judges were frequently quoted when, in sentencing a convicted person, they referred to the damage of their behaviour to Canada's war effort. But they had no apparent effect on black market activities.

About this time I had reason to drive to Montreal, where I was told that the black market in gasoline was even more widespread than in the Toronto area. Whenever I went to a service station for gasoline, the operator took a coupon from my ration book only when I insisted that he do so. One of the RCMP plainclothes men to whom I mentioned this told me about his similar experiences as he traveled about the province. In one case, when he offered his ration book to a service station operator, he was told to put it away.

"I always get into trouble when I handle one of those things," the operator explained. "I don't know the difference between genuine and counterfeit coupons."

As in the province of Quebec, the black market in gasoline coupons was common in all parts of Ontario. In Windsor, Ontario, after the RCMP there had searched a service station for counterfeit coupons, they took over the station and dispensed gasoline for an hour or so. Most of the drivers who pulled up for gasoline offered loose coupons, either genuine or counterfeit.

An investigator did not have to look for offences. He often stumbled upon them. The prevalence of gasoline rationing offences led Constables Kirkman and Wilson of the black market squad, in their usual plain clothes, into an amusing situation. After investigating some rationing offences at an industrial plant in Weston, on the outskirts of the city, they went into a nearby restaurant for a cup of coffee. As they sat at the counter a man came to the kitchen door.

"How many today, George?" he shouted at the man serving the coffee.

"Two As, three Bs, and couple of Cs," he yelled back.

Our two sleuths could only think of gasoline coupon categories, and who could blame them. When the delivery was made the man at the counter went into the kitchen, presumably to pay for the delivery. The two constables followed him.

"Alright," said one of the constables. "Where are those ration books?"

"What are you talking about?" asked the restaurant man.

"You know," said the constable. "The gasoline ration books you have just received from this fellow." He pointed to the delivery man. The restaurant man explained that the deliveries were two apple, three blueberry and two cherry pies. But the constables did not give up. They checked the gasoline ration books of the two men, and discovered that one book contained pages of counterfeit coupons, and the other a number of loose pages of genuine coupons. The constables laid charges against the men. They were later fined.

Undoubtedly gasoline rationing offences were common throughout Canada , but the Toronto black market squad was faced with more than its share of them. More cars were registered in York county, which surrounded Toronto, than in the province of Quebec, or in the three Prairie provinces combined.

TWELVE

Often, when an investigator started out on what appeared to be a simple black market investigation, he found himself involved in so many cases that he had to call on his colleagues for assistance. For instance, when Constable Barry Graham investigated the case involving the woman employee in the Oil Controller's office, he turned over some of his follow-up investigations to Constable Kirkman. He began by interviewing persons known to have bought gasoline ration coupons from her, and those who in turn had purchased coupons from them.

Most were cooperative when they realized the police had enough evidence to convict them, and this led to a number of persons about whom we had not known. It seemed that the Oil Controller's office on Spadina Avenue was a major source of black market coupons.

Through some of the people Kirkman had interviewed, he concluded that many of the coupons they had purchased originated with someone other than the convicted woman employee, but who was employed in the same office. Kirkman, being aware of how the woman employee obtained the coupons she had sold, decided to watch those now employed on the same job. These were the people who issued part-year gasoline ration books. They, like her, tore a proportionate number of coupons from the books, and placed them in containers to be taken to Hinde and Dauche to be destroyed. One would have thought that after the experience with the woman employee who was sent to jail for stealing these discarded coupons, a better system of security would now exist. Unfortunately this was not the case. As Kirkman was to see when he watched the procedures, unknown to those who did the work, the same lax methods were still in effect.

Kirkman unobtrusively observed that the coupons from the part-year ration books were thrown into cartons. At the end of the day the cartons were taken to a room and locked up for the night. It was usually a middle-aged man who took the cartons there, quite unsupervised. He stayed long enough in the room to be able to take what coupons he wanted without being seen. That particular employee, Kirkman observed, left the office more often than appeared necessary. Each time he returned in ten or fifteen minutes.

On the second day he watched from the street, and saw this employee leave the office several times. On each occasion the employee went to a nearby restaurant. There he met other men, talked to them for a few minutes, and returned to the office. Kirkman, suspicious of what was taking place, took the license numbers of the cars of those the employee had spoken to, for future inquiries.

Kirkman was never in a position to see if the employee turned over coupons to these persons, or if he just made arrangements to deliver them later, probably after office hours. Rather than spend time watching the employee's home, which could always be done later if necessary, Kirkman telephoned him at home. He said he had been told to call by a person with whom the employee had done business.

Without any questions, he arranged to meet Kirkman at the restaurant he had been seen to frequent near the office. The meeting took place as arranged. Kirkman told him he was from the west, and wanted to take as many ration coupons as he could get when he returned west in a few days. Kirkman agreed to purchase $1,000 worth, which the employee said would take several days to accumulate. At the employee's suggestion they arranged to meet three days later, at 6 p.m., in the second-floor billiard room of an old third-class hotel on Adelaide Street, just west of University Avenue. The billiard room was seldom used, the employee said, indicating that he knew the place well, and had probably used the room for the same purpose on other occasions.

Kirkman and I had plenty of time to look over the meeting place. The room faced the street, and the several windows had venetian blinds. This meant we could watch the arrival of the Oil Controller's employee. Kirkman, by manipulating the blind, could signal us as we watched from the street, when the coupons had been produced. We had no intention of passing over any money, but simply of using it as "show money", if it was necessary to encourage the employee to produce the coupons.

When we saw the signal we could rush to give him assistance if he needed it, and so make sure that he kept control of the money. We were trying to make sure that Kirkman retained the money, even if the employee took someone with him to get the $1,000 from Kirkman without producing any coupons. He would know that Kirkman, as an ordinary citizen, could hardly complain to the police.

The possible loss of the money was as much on my mind as the arrest. I told Kirkman that as soon as the coupons were produced, he should take out his revolver and hold the employee and a possible accomplice at bay while he signaled us with the venetian blinds to hasten to his assistance.

My concern about the possible loss of the $1,000 arose from the fact that some time before we had failed to find that amount, which had been paid for a used car in an over-the-ceiling-price test purchase case. To obtain authority to use this second $1,000, I convinced my superior, Inspector Schutz, that it would be used only as bait, and would not leave police hands. We were not required to make a purchase to convict the employee. His producing the coupons was sufficient for us to charge him with an offence under the Criminal Code and the Oil Controller's regulations. Reluctantly the inspector had agreed to the use of the money, but threatened, only half in fun, that if I returned without it, I might find myself on a lonely Arctic detachment.

Kirkman went to the billiard room at the appointed time, and we watchers saw the employee arrive a few minutes later, alone. Several watchers were posted at various points along the street near the hotel. I was sitting in an unmarked police car with a taxi sign in the windshield, watching the billiard room windows on the second floor. Within minutes I saw a closed venetian blind open. I flashed my car lights to alert the other watchers and we all raced into the hotel. As we entered the billiard room, I was relieved to see the $1,000 on the table, along with a stack of coupon pages. Kirkman had followed instructions to the letter, including the use of his revolver. He placed the fresh-faced, paunchy middle-aged man under arrest, and later laid a charge of breach of trust under the Criminal Code against him. The man was released on bail and suspended from his job.

A few days later Kirkman met him on the street and stopped to chat with him. Kirkman could see that the man's jacket pockets were bulging, and demanded that he empty them. The man had enough genuine pages of gasoline ration coupons to enable people to purchase tens of thousands of gallons of gasoline. He was probably on his way to make a delivery to a buyer.

Kirkman arrested him again, and this time he did not get out on bail. At his trial he pleaded guilty to the charge of breach of trust and was sentenced to two years in jail. The large number of coupons found in this man's possession indicated that he was a wholesaler, selling to others who themselves were traffickers. This man, like Glenesk, the Oil Controller's employee convicted earlier, was a former salesman. It was obvious that, when such men decided to become involved in illegal activities, they had ample associates to assist them.

After the first year of gasoline rationing, each coupon had a small empty panel in which the car owner was required to insert the license number of his car before the coupon became negotiable. This enabled black market investigators to check back on cars whose license numbers were found on coupons tendered for gasoline at service stations. In this way we found hundreds of coupons containing license numbers of cars that had never received gasoline at the service station where we found the coupons. Hence we prosecuted many service station operators, and with no difficulty at all convicted them.

In most cases it appeared that the station operators had purchased loose coupons, genuine and counterfeit, and had inserted car license numbers at random. Some license numbers were of cars owned by people living hundreds of miles from Toronto, who had never been in the city.

About this time, in an effort to have control over the service station operators, the Oil Controller set up a banking system for coupons. This required operators to open coupon bank accounts for coupons they had collected, out of which they paid the delivery man for gasoline received. The banks were supposed to keep track of all coupons deposited. This system broke down because it was impossible to keep track of the overwhelming number of coupons. While it was in effect, however, it gave a few bank clerks the opportunity of participating in the black market.

Service station owners were being charged and convicted regularly on an individual basis. In an attempt to curtail the general abuse by operators, I arranged for a one-morning blitz on service stations within the city of Toronto. The black market squad was assisted by about twenty RCMP reservists, civilians who had offered their part-time services to the RCMP during wartime.

Normally we served station operators found committing offences with summonses to appear in court at some future date. But on the blitz morning we arrested thirty-six operators immediately, for various coupon offences, and took them to jail to await bail hearings before a magistrate. Thirty-five were convicted and fined. One case was dismissed when the operator pleaded not guilty, and told a story that raised some doubt about his guilt. We knew this man had perjured himself. We investigated further, and it resulted in his conviction on a perjury charge, for which he was sentenced to six months in jail.

These cases remind me of another case arising from our search of a garage on Adelaide Street at Bay Street. We found some counterfeit coupons in the office. We had received information that stock brokers who parked their cars at the garage could purchase gasoline there without coupons. In addition to the counterfeit coupons we found other abuses. The search took place on a Friday morning. Early the following Sunday morning I received a telephone call at my home, and the caller asked to see me right away. I agreed and soon afterwards an imposing-looking Cadillac drove up to my small bungalow's front door. I opened it to let in a well-dressed middle-aged man.

He told me his name, and that he was a very senior executive of the Robert Simpson Company. He said he wanted to take responsibility for the pages of counterfeit ration coupons we had found in the Adelaide Street garage. He hadn't said that the coupons were his, but just that he would take responsibility for them. I questioned him and after a while he reluctantly admitted they were his. I was now sure that he was taking the blame for someone else, probably a higher official of the company. I accused him of this, but he denied it. Because of his position, he said, he was very embarrassed and afraid of adverse publicity, and hoped he would not be prosecuted. I explained why he had to be charged just like everyone else we found breaking wartime regulations. Later he was prosecuted and fined. As in the case of many prominent persons whose companies gave the local newspapers a great deal of advertising revenue, there was no mention in the press of his conviction. Occasionally there would be a garbled version of a conviction, with names misspelled, so that only we knew the person to whom the report really referred.

We of the black market squad tried to be fair to the people we charged with offences. I had even told my men that if ever a man needed a friend, it was when he was in the prisoner's box. I had advised them that if they could say something in favour of the accused, they should do so. They should not consider that what they said in his favour might result in less punishment, although it often did. We wanted a convicted person to be suitably punished, but in any case the punishment he received was none of our business. As I attended court, taking part in the proceedings and listening to others, I often received the impression that magistrates were always glad to hear something said in favour of the accused. It appeared that they were always looking for something on which to base a lighter sentence than would otherwise be the case.

Our attitude had some advantages. Often the accused persons appreciated the few words we said in their favour. After the cases had been disposed of, many would voluntarily give us information on black market activity, and even about ordinary criminal matters.

At times we were more than fair with accused persons, such as when defence counsel invariably asked if the accused had cooperated with us. We always answered in the affirmative, even when the accused had not cooperated at all. I could not have anticipated that the manner in which one of my men had dealt with an accused person would lead to an incident I later observed in open court.

Constable Bud Wilson had a case in which the accused had been in Canada only two years. Wilson had charged him with possession of counterfeit coupons, and he was convicted and fined. I thought the case had ended, but the accused asked if he could make a few remarks to the court. Magistrate Gullen, a kindly man, nodded, and the man began to speak in broken English. He said he had come from an eastern European country about two years earlier, a country considered a police state. When he came to Canada he had likened the police here to the police in his home country, although he did not consider Canada a police state. Nevertheless, he had maintained a fear of the police.

When he broke the law, and was charged with the current offence, he expected the police to deal harshly with him, and that he would be dealt with at least as harshly by the court. Instead, Constable Wilson had treated him like a human being, and had told him what he would face in court. The convicted man said he was glad, after a fashion, that he had broken the law, because otherwise he might have carried his false ideas of the police and the courts around with him for the rest of his life. He knew, he concluded, that he was a better Canadian for his experience.

It was not Wilson's job to do more than gather evidence, and to see that persons were appropriately charged with the offences they had committed. And he had dealt with this man as he dealt with all others. I was pleased that the incident had occurred before Magistrate Gullen, whom I had met socially on a few occasions and whom I had talked with about the RCMP black market cases flooding the Toronto courts. The magistrates did not mind the additional work, he said. He personally was glad to do it. Then he had added, "We didn't know how policemen should behave until members of the RCMP began coming to our courts."

Although one of our earliest black market cases had arisen out of Simpson's store charging above the price ceiling for a briefcase, we had left price-ceiling cases to the civilian inspectors of the Wartime Prices and Trade Board. But when a black market developed in the used-car market, it required police experience to deal with it. So we were then called upon to handle such cases.

In line with government policy to keep civilian spending at a minimum, and the need for armed services military vehicles, few new cars for civilian use came off the production lines. The scarcity of new cars created a demand for used ones, and the used-car dealers made the most of it. This forced the Vehicles Controller to set a ceiling price on all used cars, according to the year and the model. Most used-car dealers tried to evade the restrictions.

Complaints of abuses by used-car dealers were so common that we didn't have to concern ourselves about which dealer we should target. We used the test purchase method, in which a member of the black market squad pretended to be an ordinary citizen, eager to purchase a used car. He knew that the price he would have to pay for a used car was the ceiling price according to the regulations, plus the extra amount of money they demanded on the side. We also knew that a customer could get only a receipt showing the ceiling price. When the dealer was arrested by members of the black market squad other than the member who had purchased the car, we always used marked money, so that it could be retrieved from the salesman immediately after the sale.

At first these cases presented no difficulty. The marked money was always retrieved by members of the black market squad who had been watching discreetly from a distance. We had no difficulty in convicting the actual salesmen, and their companies as well.

But we ran into difficulty in one case when Constable Ted Smith, posing as an ordinary citizen, went to White Motors on Danforth Avenue, where he saw a used Buick in very good condition. The set ceiling price was marked on the car, $1650. But the salesman said the car was in such good condition that the person from whom they had obtained it had demanded over the ceiling price. Obviously, he said, he could not sell the Buick unless he raised the price. The total price for the car would be $2650, making it $1,000 over the ceiling price. Smith claimed to be taken aback by the demand for the extra money, and said he would have to think it over. Then he left the used car lot.

He returned a few hours later with $2650 in marked money which had been recorded by members of the black market squad, who now watched him go to the lot to make the deal for the Buick. When he signaled that he had done so, the watchers hastened to the lot and arrested the salesman. But when they searched him they found only $1650. They were sure Smith had paid him the full $2650, but to make sure they searched Smith, to be able to say in court that he had not retained the extra $1,000.

A shed used as an office was thoroughly searched, but the three investigators failed to find the money. They felt that it was impossible for the salesman to hide the money so that it could not be found. But they failed to find it. No one else had been on the lot to assist the salesman. He must have disposed of the $1,000 when he went into the shed office to make out the receipt for the ceiling price.

Shamefacedly I had to report to the inspector that the investigators had been unable to find the $1,000. All he said was that my investigators required a refresher course in searching small sheds used as offices. I discussed the case with the enforcement counsel of the WPTB, Mr. Dalton Wells, later Mr. Justice D.C. Wells of the Ontario Supreme Court. He agreed that we should proceed with a prosecution. Mr. J.D. Arnup, a very youthful looking, but very effective counsel, was appointed to handle the prosecution. His youthful appearance made it easy for us to call him Johnny. He later became Mr. Justice Arnup of the Ontario Supreme Court. Charges were laid against the salesman and his company, to the effect that they had sold a motor vehicle contrary to the provisions of the wartime motor vehicle regulations.

At their trials in magistrate's court they pleaded not guilty. The evidence of the police was as I have described. The defence claimed that they had received no more than the ceiling price, and the fact that the police could not find the extra $1,000 proved that they were telling the truth. The magistrate chose to believe the police, and imposed substantial fines. But the convicted parties immediately appealed their convictions.

The appeals were heard in the York County Court as trials *de novo*. This meant that the same evidence as produced in magistrate's court was heard all over again. From the beginning of this new trial, Judge Parker seemed to be annoyed at the test purchase method Ted Smith had used to buy the car. He made several caustic remarks which I thought boded ill for our case. I was not surprised when he quashed the decision of the magistrate's court.

In giving his decision he did not directly criticize the test purchase method, but he did criticize Smith's lying to the salesman about his being an ordinary civilian. "If he could lie to the salesman, he could lie when giving evidence in court," Judge Parker said in effect. In his written judgment, however, he phrased it more delicately:

> I do not think I can find on the evidence, with the weight I must attach to *agent provocateur* . . . The evidence on which I am asked to convict is the evidence of a man who goes out and confesses he deliberately lies to produce this offence. Therefore it is reasonable to expect, and I must give consideration to that phase, a man who would go out and lie to obtain an offence, how far will he go in stretching the truth to obtain a conviction? Undoubtedly he will put it in the most favourable light for the charge he has laid. That is self evident, no one will contradict that.

The term *agent provocateur* meant a police officer working under cover in order to put a stop to an ongoing crime. This was exactly what Ted Smith had done in his capacity as a police constable. Judge Parker, apparently, had given the term its literal meaning, the provoking of a crime when none existed. There was ample jurisprudence to support the manner in which Smith had gone about his duties.

Normally a decision of a County court, trying a summary conviction case *de novo*, was the final one from which there was no appeal. Fortunately, the Wartime Prices and Trade Board regulations provided for an appeal to the Supreme Court of a province in such cases. There was only one thing to do – appeal Judge Parker's decision to the Supreme Court of Ontario.

*T*HIRTEEN

Failure to appeal Judge Parker's ruling would have created quite a stir in the law enforcement field. It would have been only a short time until his judgment was being referred to all over Canada. This would have affected not only the enforcement of the wartime regulations, but also the enforcement of the drug laws in which undercover RCMP members, under the guise of addicts or others associated with the illicit drug trade, constantly made test purchases of illicit drugs.

Prosecutor Johnny Arnup had no difficulty in getting the Wartime Prices and Trade Board to agree to an appeal, since without the test purchase method, enforcement of the wartime rationing regulations would be seriously impeded.

First the Crown had to seek leave to appeal to the Supreme Court of Ontario. At this hearing, J.A. Laidlaw, commenting on the points raised in the application, said:

> With much respect, I am of the opinion that the learned judge [Parker] improperly discredited the police constable. I can see no reason to criticize his conduct in any way, but, on the contrary, am impressed with the view that he was carrying out his duty as an officer of the law in a proper and necessary manner under circumstances . . . Indeed, it would be difficult, if not impossible, for officers of the law to prevent or successfully combat certain kinds of crime (including offences charged against

the accused), except by the employment of measures involving masquerade, deceit and false representation.

Mr. Justice Laidlaw supported his opinion by referring to rulings in the British courts over a period of more than a hundred years. Leave to appeal was granted. I was especially pleased that the leave to appeal was based on the correctness of the police action in the purchase of the used car.

Three judges sat on the appeal. Johnny Arnup had prepared himself well with jurisprudence also stretching over more than a century. In his presentation he questioned a point implicit in the decision of Judge Parker, that an undercover policeman's evidence should be corroborated. Several British appeal judges had ruled on this same point. Mr. Justice Erle, stated in 1909:

> If he only lent himself to the scheme for the purpose of convicting the guilty, he was a good witness and his testimony did not require confirmation as that of an accomplice would do . . .

This was one problem Judge Parker might have had with Ted Smith's evidence.

All three Justices referred to the same jurisprudence in making their separate decisions. They showed that for a century and a half the Crown had been fighting in the courts the suggestion that police undercover agents had enticed people to break the law, whereas such agents merely joined conspiracies to bring them to an end. From such cases, the term *agent provocateur,* in its adverse sense, had arisen quite improperly. The term originated in France about the mid-18th Century. It was linked closely to persons who resorted to the then common practice of encouraging, procuring or counselling others to commit actions against the state. In those days anyone who could be persuaded to commit such an offence was an enemy of the state and could be harshly punished as such. At that time the term *agent provocateur* was properly applied to those who provoked others to commit offences which they would not otherwise have committed. The term would also properly apply today to a policeman who enticed innocent people to commit crimes.

The term, however, in its disparaging sense, came to be applied to police undercover men who worked within a criminal conspiracy to bring it to an end. It began, most likely, when defence counsel, as they still do, accused undercover policemen of provoking their innocent clients to commit crimes which would otherwise not have been committed. Fortunately, our courts see the difference between those to whom the term could properly be applied, and the police acting to bring continuing crime to an end.

The unanimous decision of the Supreme Court was that the case should be sent back to Judge Parker's County court again to be tried *de novo*. At that time the judge would have to accept the Supreme Court's views on the points in Ted Smith's evidence to which he had objected. The new hearing was dealt with rather expediently, and both the company and its salesman were found guilty. The moderate fines meted out undoubtedly reflected the judge's repugnance toward the methods used by the police in enforcing wartime regulations. But as far as I was concerned, acceptance of the police use of the test purchase method was far more important.

We encountered Judge Parker again when a Windsor man was convicted in a Toronto magistrate's court for trafficking in gasoline ration coupons. The evidence against him included the evidence of an undercover policeman making a test purchase. The convicted man appealed, and the trial *de novo* was again before Judge Parker. This time he registered a conviction, but he clearly showed his distaste for the method used by the police to secure evidence. He imposed only a moderate fine. Fortunately we seldom ran into judges with the views of Judge Parker. But I began to think that when they became known, we were likely to see many more appeals before him, not necessarily to have the charges dismissed, but to lessen the punishment meted out in the magistrate's court. But there were no further appeals to Judge Parker's court, and none to other judges in the York County Court.

One could always find a little drama in the courts if one looked for it. With so many prosecutions under the wartime regulations, some members of the RCMP black market squad were in court nearly every working day. One day while I was waiting for my case to be heard, I listened to a case of Constable Kirkman's. It concerned a young Chinese restaurateur's possession of several pages of four-coupon counterfeit pages that had been inserted in his gasoline ration book. Kirkman had investigated the case and laid the necessary charge against the young man. Mr. Joseph Singer, K.C. was appointed to prosecute. He was probably the shrewdest counsel the government had appointed to handle our cases. If I had ever been charged with an offence, I would have wanted Mr. Singer to defend me. We were fortunate that his talents were used on our behalf.

The young man was charged with possessing counterfeit ration coupons. The case was a simple one. Kirkman gave evidence of his finding the counterfeit coupons in the young man's gasoline ration book. That's all there is to it, I thought, but the defence counsel had other ideas. He called the accused to the witness box to tell his story. His father, he said, had died about six months before, leaving him the restaurant and a car. The ration book came with the car and the counterfeit coupons, without his knowledge, were in it. There was no evidence to disprove his story. That's it I now thought, there's enough doubt about which the accused should be given the benefit. I expected the magistrate to dismiss the case right there.

But defence counsel could not leave well enough alone. He called the accused's mother to give character evidence, and to corroborate her son's story about his father's death. She gave her evidence in Chinese through an interpreter. Yes, it was true, her husband had died six months before, leaving the business and the car to his son. Yes, he was a good son, a good businessman and very honest, and he looked after her as well as she could possibly wish. Again, I thought, the case should be dismissed immediately.

Then Mr. Singer stood up to cross-examine the old lady. Slowly he asked about where she lived, how long she had been in Canada, and how many children she had. Then he questioned her about her late husband, the years they had been married, and where else in Canada they had lived besides Toronto. I was getting annoyed at Mr. Singer. This kind of questioning was not getting anyone anywhere, and I was tired of waiting for my case to be heard.

But he continued. Was her husband an honest man? Yes, of course. And had he purchased plenty of war bonds to prove it? Now it seemed to me there was some purpose to Mr. Singer's questions. Had her husband ever been convicted of any offence during the years he had been in Canada?

"Never," she answered slowly, through the interpreter.

Then came a question which made her hesitate. Was her husband the kind of man who, in the middle of a war, would damage Canada's war effort by dealing in counterfeit coupons just so that he could drive his car more than the government wanted him to?

He had to repeat the long question, and as he did so she stared at her son. She had caught the drift of the question, and did not know what to answer. If she said, yes, all she had said about her husband's honesty and patriotism would seem false. If she said no, that meant that her son must have acquired the counterfeit coupons himself. She hesitated for some minutes as those in the court became aware of her dilemma. Her answer would free or convict her son. At last she answered the last question by whispering a reluctant no. Mr. Singer sat down.

Magistrate Prentice did not ask for any comment from defence counsel. "Fifty dollars or thirty days," he said. It was just a simple case, but it had drama.

There could also be a certain amount of drama outside the courtroom. During my investigation of a gasoline rationing case in a small town north of Toronto, I learned that the local church minister had used loose coupons to purchase gasoline. I went to his home and in the presence of his wife asked him if this was true. Sheepishly he admitted it. At my request he produced his ration book, and I found about a dozen genuine loose coupons in it. By now he was extremely embarrassed. He had visions of appearing in magistrate's court charged with offences against wartime regulations. He dreaded the effect it would have on his congregations.

By way of explanation he told me that he was not only the minister of the church in that town, but also in two other widely separated and smaller congregations out in the country. His ration allotment was not sufficient to allow him to visit his outlying congregations with any regularity. So a few of them had given him a loose coupon or two. He gave me their names and addresses, and I went to see them. They admitted they had given the preacher some coupons. I pointed out that they had broken the law, which they already knew.

On my way back to the small town in which the minister lived, I concluded that the abuse of the regulations in this case was not great, and that it had been done for a good purpose. I thought that if there were a place for the use of police discretion, this was it. I called at the minister's home, and told him I was not going to lay a charge against him, but I would have to take possession of the loose coupons he had. It is impossible to describe his and his wife's relief. Before I told him, he was one person, and afterwards a completely different one. He broke down and cried with relief. I realized then that if I had laid a charge against him, his punishment would have been far greater than anything imposed by a court on the average citizen.

At the same time I wondered how many ministers in Canada were purchasing gasoline on the black market with coupons provided by their parishioners.

FOURTEEN

There were probably many hundreds of officials dealing with the public in relation to the wartime regulations, so I would have been naive to think that those we prosecuted in and around Toronto were the only ones abusing them. Similar opportunities existed in hundreds of government offices enforcing the regulations from coast to coast.

The Commodity Prices Stabilization Corporation (CPSC), a government department, paid subsidies to certain industries so that the retail ceiling price of their products could remain as set by the government. No subsidy was paid, however, before an inspector investigated the merits of a claim.

Because car and truck tires were rationed, there was a demand for old worn-out tires that could be retreaded. Some companies collected old tires. They sold the ones that could be retreaded and reclaimed rubber from the others. These companies were also forced to sell used tires within the ceiling price. But often, unless they were granted a subsidy, they would operate at a loss. When an inspector of the corporation investigated a subsidy claim of the National Rubber Company in Toronto, he found the subsidy was not warranted. The two brothers who owned the company offered the inspector $1,000 to approve their claim.

The inspector, with the approval of the chief inspector of the corporation, reported the bribe offer to the RCMP, and then handed it over to the black market squad for investigation. I thought at the time that as a purely criminal matter of bribery it was a CIB matter. The inspector told me that the bribe offer had taken place in the company's office, with only himself and the two brothers present. Instead of rejecting the bribe he had told them that he would think it over, and then reported the attempted bribe to the chief inspector in Ottawa.

He seemed pleased to be involved in such a matter, and instantly agreed to play along with the brothers under our supervision, to try to develop enough evidence on which to base a prosecution against them. He obviously had a fertile imagination, and made a number of inappropriate suggestions as to how we could trap the brothers. I soon realized that our close supervision was vital.

"You must keep a notebook," I told him. "As soon as possible after meeting with the brothers you must record everything that was said, and include both the date and time of day. I will check your notes every day to make sure they are properly kept."

Although the inspector met the brothers at places outside their office, they would only discuss the offer of the $1,000 in the safety of their office. After a while we concluded there was little hope of obtaining corroboration of the bribe offer. In an attempt to get it we even went so far as to have the inspector feign a badly injured leg, so that we could entice the brothers to visit his room in the *Royal York* hotel, where he stayed when he was in Toronto. We had "bugged" the room earlier and were ready next door to record any incriminating conversation.

When the brothers visited their ailing "friend", they were careful not to say anything that would link them with the attempted bribe, even though the inspector tried to get them into conversation about it by asking them when he could expect the money they had promised to pay him. The fact that they didn't ask him what he was talking about was only the mildest corroboration that a bribe offer had taken place.

It appeared to me that the only thing we could do to conclude the matter was for the investigator to make an outright request for the $1,000 they had offered him. He visited their office every few days under the pretence of looking over their books. At last I told him to ask directly for the money they had promised him, and to say that he had no intention of recommending a subsidy until they paid it. We knew this approach would not look good if the matter went to court. But there was nothing else we could do.

Before the visit during which the inspector would ask for money, we searched him to make sure that he had no money on him other than what he had in his wallet. We then watched while he went directly to the company's office, and again later when he left the office and returned to us. He explained that he didn't have the bribe money, however. The brothers had offered only to give him $500 on his next visit. On that next visit we repeated the search procedure, and found when he left the office he had $500 more than when he entered the company's office. But even this did not make an airtight case. The brothers could always say the inspector had asked for a loan and they had given it to him. We still needed more evidence before laying a charge. We had decided, after the inspector was paid the second $500, to seize the company's books of account to show that the subsidy they had applied for was not warranted. Meanwhile I continued to check his notebook daily.

Then we ran into difficulties with the inspector's superior, the chief inspector, who thought enough time had been spent on the investigation. He withdrew his inspector's cooperation. Nevertheless we seized the company's books of account. Later I placed the evidence we had against the two brothers before a special prosecutor appointed by the federal government. He recommended a prosecution. I was pleased to lay the charges but I was not optimistic about a conviction.

The trial was held before a judge and jury. The evidence we were prepared to produce included the inspector's story of being offered a bribe; the reaction of the brothers' request for money in the hotel room; RCMP observations at the time he was given $500 on account; and the testimony of an accountant that would show the company was not entitled to a subsidy. On paper it seemed like a fairly good case, but much of the evidence we were prepared to present was never given. The inspector, notebook in hand, took the stand. I had checked the notebook the previous evening, and had gone over his evidence with him. He gave that evidence in a very satisfactory manner, occasionally referring to his notebook to support his story. Then defence counsel, Mr. (later senator) Salter Hayden, began to cross-examine him. Everything went well until the inspector couldn't answer a question, even though he referred to his notebook.

"Oh, that must be in the other notebook," he said. My heart sank. I knew the fat was in the fire.

"What other notebook?" asked Mr. Hayden.

Then the witness explained that after checking his notes with me the previous evening, he decided they were too messy, so he had rewritten them in a nice new clean notebook.

"Where is the other notebook?" Mr. Hayden asked.

"I destroyed it," the inspector answered meekly.

The fact that the inspector's evidence had been based chiefly on secondhand notes brought the case to an abrupt end. Without his credible evidence we had no case. Although I was saddened by the turn of events, I was not sorry to see the end of the matter.

In pondering why the chief inspector had impeded the investigation in such an arbitrary way, by removing his inspector, I concluded it was linked to an incident during the latter stages of the investigation. He had telephoned me and demanded, in an upper class English accent, that I go immediately to his room at the *Royal York* hotel. His imperious manner on the telephone alerted me to the advisability of taking Constable Barry Graham with me as a witness.

As we entered his hotel room I noticed that he seemed annoyed.

"I thought I could speak to you alone," he said.

"About what?" I asked.

"I have been informed that one of your investigators has seized some counterfeit gas ration coupons from the man in charge of my Toronto office, and that a prosecution is pending."

"I am fully aware of the case," I responded. "But why are you so upset about it."

"I don't think it's proper," he said, "that when two departments have worked as closely as we have done, (meaning the bribery case) that one should go about laying charges against employees of the other."

This was a one-way business, because we could lay charges against his employees for infractions against the rationing regulations, but the RCMP was hardly in the business of claiming subsidies from his corporation. Obviously agitated, he paced the room.

"I want you to withdraw the charges against my employee," he demanded, as if there could be no doubt about his being obeyed.

"I can't do that. As a former bank manager he should know better than to involve himself in the black market," I responded with some heat. My answer infuriated him.

"If you don't do it, I'll see that none of my investigators will ever again assist the RCMP," he shouted.

I couldn't believe my ears. This was my first meeting with him, but it hadn't taken me long to realize that he was one of the kind of pompous and arrogant Englishmen that make themselves unpopular in Canada. He gave the impression that we "colonials" owed him a great debt for the help he was giving Canada in its war effort. He had been in Canada only a relatively short time, and certainly did not appreciate the part the RCMP played in the general enforcement of Canada's laws. At that point I left the room with Constable Graham, who had watched the chief inspector's behaviour with amazement.

We returned to the office and I immediately typed a report describing in detail what had taken place, including the chief inspector's threat never again to allow anyone from his department to assist the RCMP. In conclusion I suggested that if he were ever interviewed by a member of the RCMP, because of the type of man he might be, it should only be done in the presence of a witness.

I had half forgotten the matter when, a few weeks later, I was instructed to go to Ottawa and present myself to the RCMP deputy commissioner at a certain time and date. No reason was given. When I arrived at his office I found him reading my report. He handed it to me and wanted to know if I wanted to change anything in it. I read the report and handed it back to him.

"I don't want to withdraw a single word, sir."

Then he told me to return in half an hour to discuss the report with the chief inspector of the CPSC. Before I left he told me that the meeting was to be held at the express wish of Commissioner S.T. Wood and Mr. Hector McKinnon, the chief inspector's superior and a well-known senior civil servant. By the time I returned the chief inspector was already there, reading his own copy of my report. The three of us went over it, paragraph by paragraph. As he agreed with most of what I had reported, I wondered what was the purpose of our meeting. Then we came to the place where I had said, "in view of the type of man [the chief inspector] might be," he should be dealt with only in presence of a witness.

"That's libel!" he shouted, his temper flaring as it had done in the hotel room in Toronto.

The deputy commissioner looked at me for my reaction.

"My report says exactly what I mean," I said. "After my experience with him in his hotel room, I would not want to interview him on any matter without a witness being present. If that's libel, so be it."

It took some time for the Chief Inspector to settle down. Then the discussion turned to his calling his inspector off the bribery case. He denied having done it. Fortunately, he had done so by telephoning to my office, where he had expected to find his inspector. When he learned that his inspector was not there, he spoke instead to another of his inspectors who had come to the office to see the inspector in the bribery case. The other inspector was Max Fell, who had been in charge of the Toronto Foreign Exchange Control Board's investigative group of which I had been temporarily a member, while we worked on a gold smuggling case a year or so earlier.

I suggested to the deputy commissioner that the matter could be clarified quite easily, since Mr. Fell was still employed under the chief inspector, in his Ottawa office. A telephone call would give us the answer. I felt sure Fell would remember because he had been very incensed at the action taken by his chief inspector. The deputy commissioner telephoned Fell who told him that he remembered the chief inspector's call quite well, and that he was told by him to tell the bribery inspector that cooperation with the RCMP should cease forthwith.

By now the deputy commissioner had had enough. He wanted to bring the meeting to an end. But the chief inspector would not have it. He transferred his venom from me to the deputy commissioner.

"Of course," he said, "I could hardly expect anything else but that a deputy commissioner would protect one of his subordinates."

I was only a lowly detective sergeant, and this was my first meeting with anyone of such an exalted rank as a deputy commissioner. I believed that if I had done anything wrong I would have had "the book" thrown at me. I sat back in my chair, inwardly chuckling while they shouted at each other. The chief inspector himself was demonstrating to the deputy commissioner what I had tried to convey in my report, as to why he should never be interviewed without a witness being present.

About three years later, after I had been commissioned as a sub-inspector and transferred to Ottawa, the deputy commissioner told me how it came about that he had called me to Ottawa after receiving my report on my first interview with the chief inspector. Commissioner Wood had sent a copy of it to his friend, Mr. Hector McKinnon, head of Commodity Prices Stabilization Corporation and the chief inspector's superior. Mr. McKinnon had supported the chief inspector's demand for a face-to-face meeting with me in the presence of the deputy commissioner. After this meeting took place Commissioner Wood wrote to Mr. McKinnon. He declared that as long as the chief inspector was in charge of investigations for his corporation, he could not expect any assistance from the RCMP. A few months later the chief inspector resigned from the corporation.

I had never been involved in anything like this before, and certainly not since. I was pleased to see that members of the Force would be supported from on high if they were in the right, every bit as much as I knew they would be jumped on from the same height if they were in the wrong.

FIFTEEN

The men of the RCMP Reserve were of great assistance, not only to the black market squad, but also to the RCMP Special Branch, especially when the latter had the responsibility of rounding up suspected subversives after war was declared in September 1939. They helped again nine months later, in June 1940, at which time Mussolini joined Hitler, and the Canadian government ordered the internment of certain Canadian pro-fascists.

The reserve, made up of civilians from all levels of society, included truck drivers, doctors, lawyers, bankers, stockbrokers and various businessmen. The reservists, who took drill practice and lectures once or twice a week, received the basic brown uniform, including the RCMP peak cap, and held the rank of reserve constable. They were given no pay, and were active mostly in Toronto and Montreal.

In Toronto their "home" was a large hall in the post office building at Queen and Saulter streets. But in Montreal, where the reservists were even more active, they made use of the officers' mess in the RCMP divisional headquarters building. There, after a stint of duty, they went to the mess to refresh themselves and to talk about their experiences. Some of their stories reached Toronto, and a few of them have always stood out in my memory.

One of these began the day the Red Cross asked the commanding officer in Montreal if he could send some men to the Windsor station, to help that organization with a trainload of refugees and other overseas people. The train had just arrived from an eastern Canadian port, as Halifax was referred to during the war. The C.O. called upon a number of reservists, and they hastened to help out at the station. In their dull brown uniforms they looked like station porters.

One reservist helped an elderly English gentleman by carrying his bag out of the station and finding him a taxi. Before getting into the taxi the Englishman pulled out his purse, searched among the coins, and handed his "porter" a shilling. The "porter" returned to the RCMP mess with his new-found wealth, much to the amusement of the other reservists. The next day, in his capacity as a financier, he attended a meeting with a group of financiers from England who had come to Canada to negotiate a huge loan. Among them was the man who had given him the shilling, but the English visitor did not recognize his "porter" of the previous day, nor did the RCMP reservist identify himself. The Canadian banker framed his shilling and hung it in his office. After that he referred to himself as "a-shilling-a-war" man as opposed to the "dollar-a-year" men employed by the federal government in Ottawa.

Another story concerned a well-known dentist in Montreal, brother of a famous lawyer who later became a Justice of the Supreme Court of Canada. The RCMP called the dentist for duty, and gave him the job of guarding a gate at the dockyards. During his duty there, a man who said he had business with a high authority inside the gates tried to gain entrance without showing the necessary pass. The reserve constable explained that the man couldn't enter without a pass, which he could get at the office outside the gate. The visitor identified himself as a high official of a local company, but the reserve constable insisted he must get a pass. Very annoyed, the man went back to the office and obtained one.

After he passed through the gate, he turned around and asked the reservist what rank he held.

"Reserve Constable, sir," was the polite answer.

"And a man as stupid as you will always be a reserve constable," the visitor retorted angrily. Another tale for the officers' mess.

Later in the war the reserve constables from Toronto and Montreal were detailed for duty in Quebec City. There they helped with the security of Prime Ministers Winston Churchill and W.L. McKenzie King, when Churchill visited Quebec City after his conference with President Roosevelt aboard a U.S. warship off Newfoundland. One evening the RCMP corporal in charge of the security detail noticed that a reservist had appeared on duty improperly dressed. The corporal ordered him to report to the sergeant major's office at a certain time the next morning.

"I'm afraid I can't do that, corporal," the reservist answered politely.

"And why not?" bellowed the surprised corporal.

"Because I have an appointment at that time to see Prime Minister Churchill. You see, when we were boys we went to school together, and he asked to see me."

Meanwhile, my own career was progressing favourably. Since arriving in Toronto in October 1939, from a rural detachment in Saskatchewan, my work had been suitably recognized each year, and I had been promoted faster than the average member. I was to stay in the division seven years, and I received promotion of one kind or another in all of them except one. I attributed much of my success, not only to a lot of hard work, but also to luck in being in the right place at the right time.

An example of the latter category occurred one evening in March 1942, while I was still a detective corporal. I was attending a lecture at the Beverly Street barracks, one of many the C.O. arranged throughout the war years. In the middle of the lecture someone came in and whispered to the C.O. He immediately named several men, me included, and we followed him into the barracks hall.

Earlier that evening, he told us, someone had attempted to derail the Chicago Flyer, a fast train between Chicago and Toronto. The attempt had been made at a switching point near Cooksville, a few miles west of Toronto. The C.O. then detailed five of us to go to the scene of the attempted derailment with the corporal in charge of the Civil Security branch, the branch responsible for industrial security. One of the five was the branch member who two weeks before had investigated, without result, an earlier attempt to derail the same train at the same switching point near Cooksville.

This second attempt to derail the Flyer, like the first one, brought men of several police forces to the scene. A cavalcade of cars carried representatives of the Toronto Township Police, the CPR police, the Ontario Provincial Police, the RCMP and, as seemed strange to me, the Toronto city police.

I was annoyed at being a part of this small army sent out to do what I considered a one- or two-man job. I had plenty of work in my own sphere of responsibility, black market, without being involved in work so clearly the responsibility of the RCMP Civil Security Branch. On our drive out, the Civil Security Branch member who had investigated the previous incident told us what had happened at that time. The engineer of the Flyer had noticed something wrong with the switch signal light, enough to warn him to bring the train to a halt. He discovered that the switch had been turned halfway to the full red light position, and the switch lock was missing. It was clear to him that someone had tried to force the switch full open, in an attempt to derail the train. As he came to a halt, the engineer thought he saw a figure running away from the railroad, but as it was dark he could not be sure. He looked around and found the lock, but there was no sign of the chain. He then closed the switch and drove the train into Toronto, where he reported the matter to the CPR police, who in turn notified the RCMP.

The police had begun to investigate immediately, and the next day had even taken a police tracking dog to the scene. The dog led them to some Nazi drawings in the snow, and then to a side road, where he lost the trail. The swastika drawings gave the police cause to think that the incident involved sabotage, although the attempted derailment seemed a rather amateurish effort. The subsequent investigation had not resulted in the police finding any leads that would help them find the culprit. They hoped for better success on this second occasion.

It was nearly midnight when our cavalcade arrived at a side road about a half mile from the railroad switch that had been tampered with. Lightly falling snow had covered the surrounding fields, but the snow that fell on the warmer asphalt had melted, exposing a long black road through a wide open expanse of snow-covered fields on either side. The investigating party agreed to walk to the switch, leaving the cars parked on the highway. Obviously not all of us were required at the switch so I volunteered, along with Constables Lindsay and Hanna of the RCMP, to guard the cars while the others walked to the switch.

Before long, Lindsay, Hanna and I got tired of waiting for the investigators to return. Lindsay suggested, somewhat jokingly, that we walk along the highway to see if we could find some tracks in the snow, leading from the direction of the railroad switch. Leaving Hanna to look after the cars, Lindsay and I set out. There was no moon that night, but the clean snow gave us plenty of light. About three hundred yards from the parked cars we saw man-sized footprints in the field, coming from the general direction of the railroad. They disappeared when they reached the wet highway.

We kept on walking, found them again on the other side of the highway, and then followed them to a well-lighted farmhouse about half a mile away. On the lighted back verandah we found a pair of large wet rubber boots. We took them back to the tracks and found that they fitted perfectly. It seemed clear that the owner had recently come from the direction of the railroad, if not from the switch itself. We returned to the farmhouse and knocked on the screen door.

Through the screen we saw a man come into the well-lighted kitchen, and we introduced ourselves to him as members of the RCMP. When we produced the rubber boots we had picked up on the verandah, he invited us inside.

"They belong to my hired hand," he said. "Is there anything wrong?"

We told him about the attempt to derail the Flyer, and the tracks which appeared to come from the railroad, apparently made by the person who had worn the rubber boots. The farmer said that he had heard his hired man come home some hours earlier, and that he had gone upstairs to bed. He gave us permission to go upstairs to speak to him.

The farmer led us to his hired man's bedroom in the attic, and switched on the light. The hired man, an Indian lad about sixteen years of age, pretended to be asleep, but we had already seen him with his eyes open when his employer switched on the light. He got out of bed and followed us down to the kitchen.

"If you don't tell the truth, I'll break your bloody neck," the farmer threatened.

The youth admitted that a couple of weeks earlier he had tried to open the switch, but had been able to open it only part way. When he had seen the train coming he ran into a nearby field. He had seen the engineer stop the train, get off the engine, close the switch, and take the train through it slowly. The youth had returned to the switch after the train had gone and had drawn swastikas in the snow.

On this second attempt he had gone to the switch after supper, and thought he had succeeded in opening it. He again watched from a distance and saw the train stop. Obviously, the engineer had seen a red light instead of the expected white, and knew the switch was open. The youth presumed the engineer had closed the switch because the train had gone on toward Toronto. Then he went back to a place near the switch and again drew swastikas in the snow.

I took a long written statement from him, and had it witnessed by the farmer and Constable Lindsay. Placing the youth under arrest, we searched his room. We found a notebook full of drawings of swastikas and written "Heil Hitlers", a cover from a switch lock, and the chain that had fastened the lock to the railway switch. Taking our prisoner with us, we walked back to the parked police cars.

As the "investigators" had not returned, we put the youth in the back seat of an RCMP car and waited for them. In about half an hour they turned up, and I encouraged them to tell us all they had discovered. They had found a footprint and had covered it with a carton so that a plaster cast could be taken later that morning. They also had found drawings of Nazi swastikas in the snow, but nothing more. I was surprised that they hadn't found rubber boot tracks leading from the switch, but I guessed that the Indian lad had walked some distance down the railway track before crossing the snowy field on his way home.

I led the RCMP corporal to the police car in which the prisoner sat, and turned my flashlight on him. A great commotion ensued. Everybody clamoured to know where he had come from. I produced his written statement and then everyone wanted to read it. Soon, however, I had to take it from them because the still softly falling snow was smudging the ink.

Our cavalcade returned to Toronto in the early morning hours, and I put the prisoner in a city police station cell, pending his appearance in a Brampton Court later that day. When he appeared before the magistrate the case was adjourned for a week, during which we charged him with two offences of Displacing a Railroad Switch contrary to Section 282 (a) of the Criminal Code.

As the case was being handled by the RCMP Civil Security branch, I handed the youth's statement to the corporal in charge, so that he could embody it in his report. Later that morning I was telling the senior crime report reader at divisional headquarters what had happened the night before.

"That's strange," he said. "I received the corporal's report early this morning and there's no mention of you or Lindsay being involved in the taking of the statement or in making the arrest. I have passed the report to Inspector Schutz."

I was more than annoyed that Constable Lindsay, with more years of service than I, and still a constable, was being denied the credit he deserved. Certainly, if it had not been for his initiative we might never have solved the case. I realized then that I should have kept the statement and put in the report myself.

I immediately typed a report covering the facts as I knew them. Then I took it to the office of Inspector Schutz, who had the corporal's report on his desk. He read my report and then said, "Leave the matter with me. I'll attend to it."

The next day the senior crime report reader told me that my report had been handed to the corporal so that all the facts could be embodied in the report that would be sent to headquarters in Ottawa. Later, I read the report and saw that Lindsay had received due credit for his initiative. As for me, my part in the incident was duly noted, but, as on other occasions, it was just a matter of my being in the right place at the right time. Two weeks later the youth pleaded guilty to two charges, and was sentenced to eighteen months in jail.

As the Toronto black market squad continued to investigate the trafficking in gasoline ration coupons, both genuine and counterfeit, we continued to prosecute the traffickers and the service station operators. Many of the latter were not only dispensing gasoline for loose coupons, but also were supplying it for an extra charge of five to ten cents a gallon when the car owner had no coupons at all. These operators told black market members, working undercover, that they used the extra charge to pay for the coupons they purchased to pass on to their gasoline suppliers.

Traffickers were charging car owners as much as fifty cents a coupon, for coupons which had been obtained from ration books they had stolen. This lucrative business encouraged traffickers to break into ration book issuing offices and the offices of fleet truck owners. In the latter case, not only the number of books attracted the thieves, but the fact that they were the large commercial ones. In the late winter of 1943-44, just before the beginning of the 1944 rationing year, 3,500 AA category books were stolen from the issuing office of the Ontario Motor League on Bay Street in Toronto. We estimated that another 2,000 ration books were stolen from various other offices in southern Ontario. AA books were being sold for between five and ten dollars, and higher categories for sometimes as high as fifty dollars.

SIXTEEN

The plant of Rolph, Clark Stone, the company with the contract to print all gasoline ration coupons, continued for a time to be a source of illegal ration coupons. Four sheets of 280 coupons each came off the presses at one time. The company cut them down into four-coupon pages, which they made into books of various categories. Thieves, with the connivance of some plant employees, stole hundreds of uncut sheets, and then sold them to traffickers for from fifteen to twenty dollars each. They were then resold for from thirty to forty dollars a sheet to others who cut them to page size, and sold them to car owners for one dollar or more a page.

Ration books were issued by the various offices throughout Canada. Then they passed through the hands of car owners, service station operators, gasoline delivery truck drivers, oil company workers and those who operated used coupon destruction facilities. The opportunities to abuse the rationing regulations were unlimited. We prosecuted people at every level. So many coupons changed hands that a proper accounting was impossible. There came a time when I knew that all the black market squad could do was to try and limit abuses by prosecuting as many people as possible, to keep the abuses to a minimum. Even at that we seldom had time to worry about abuses by individual car owners.

The gasoline rationing system, to work effectively, depended upon the honesty of all those who handled ration coupons, from the point of issue to their destruction, but especially at the service station level. There gasoline should have only been dispensed on the presentation of genuine gasoline books, issued for the car receiving the gasoline. Service station operators were required to tear the coupon from the ration book.

A half-hearted attempt to have some control over abuses at the service station level took place when the Oil Controller ordered operators to stamp their names and addresses on the backs of coupons they claimed they had taken for gasoline supplied. They simply stamped all the coupons they had, whether from legal ration books or coupons purchased from traffickers.

When rampant dishonesty was so obvious, the Oil Controller initiated a gasoline ration coupon banking system, in an effort to make service station operators and oil companies more accountable for the loose used coupons they handled. This attacked only part of the problem. Then the Oil Controller ordered that ration coupons include a small empty panel, in which the car owner had to write his car license number, but it did little to stop abuses. Service station operators continued to purchase illegal coupons, and filled in any license numbers that came to mind. This requirement did, however, work to the advantage of the black market squad. We could check with the owner of the car, whose license number was on a coupon we had found at the service station. When we did so, more often than not, we found that he had not purchased gasoline at the service station concerned.

Under the banking system, each station operator deposited his used coupons into his bank account. When he received a supply of gasoline he issued a cheque on his account. But there were so many coupons deposited in banks that the banks couldn't be expected to count all the coupons deposited. At least one bank employee was convicted for helping himself to deposited coupons. The black market squad spent some time examining the deposited coupons. It was no surprise when we found coupons with license numbers, in the small panels, of cars that had never been supplied with gasoline in the Toronto area. The license numbers had been entered indiscriminately by station operators on coupons purchased from traffickers.

Our examination also revealed large numbers of counterfeit coupons. Hence more prosecutions.

As early as the end of the first rationing year, counterfeit coupons began to appear. The next year Toronto was flooded with four-coupon counterfeit pages for insertion in the genuine ration books. In one case we seized 2,000 pages and arrested five men who were associated with their distribution. From that time until the end of gasoline rationing, in the spring of 1945, we sent samples of every coupon seizure to the RCMP crime laboratory in Rockcliffe, Ontario, where document examiners checked them. By the end of gasoline rationing they had reported ten to twelve different types of counterfeit coupons. That meant there were many illegal presses turning them out.

It became impossible for the ten-man black market squad in Toronto to do any more than scratch the surface in bringing gasoline rationing offenders before the courts. I could only assume that the same abuses were taking place all over Canada, and that the gasoline rationing system was being sabotaged by black marketeers and other criminals. I was sure that I was not the only one who believed that gasoline rationing was out of control.

In the meantime, the government authorities were designing different gasoline ration coupons each year, which made their counterfeiting more difficult. But when rationing ended in the spring of 1945, the latest counterfeit coupons, ready for the new rationing year, were so perfectly printed that no ordinary person could distinguish the genuine from the counterfeit coupons.

In the case in which genuine gasoline ration books had been stolen from the Ontario Motor League on Bay Street in Toronto, one of my men made the most spectacular arrest I have ever seen. A well-known petty criminal had told one of my informants that he had a supply of the stolen books. At my request, the informant agreed to try to buy some of them, on the understanding that if successful we would arrest the criminal before he came into contact with the informant.

The informant made a deal for the purchase of fifty ration books, and on my advice he told the criminal that he would take delivery of them on a short, quiet street behind the Toronto General Hospital. He would be parked in his car waiting for the delivery at a certain time. The street block chosen had houses on the west side, and a vacant lot on the other. On the far side from the street, the vacant lot was enclosed by a high board fence This I thought would hold back the suspect until we reached him, if he attempted to escape by running in that direction.

To prevent his escape by car, I had arranged for two old vans, driven by members of the Force, to be at each end of the block on the streets that ran at right angles to the street where the informant was to park his car. If the suspect decided to escape by car, on a signal from me, at the foot of the block in a car with a taxi sign, the two vans could close the street and prevent the escaping car from leaving. Another member of the Force, Constable McIver, dressed in very old clothes, was feigning sleep on the steps of one of the houses near where the informant would park. Two other members of the Force, appropriately dressed, had driven an old unmarked police car onto the vacant lot. With the hood up they pretended to be working on the motor.

We were all in place when the informant drove up and parked at the selected place. Shortly afterwards the suspect drove into the north end of the street and parked about three car lengths behind the informant. For several minutes he made no effort to leave his car, no doubt surveying the surroundings before deciding it was safe to do so. I was sure we had him in a trap, except that he might escape by running across the vacant lot and climbing over the fence. The two men working on their car were to prevent his escape by this route. All my men were situated so that they could see the prearranged signal of my flicking car lights.

After the suspect had opened his car door, and had one foot on the ground, I signaled. The two vans moved into place, and the men started to run toward the suspect. Rather than run toward him, the two car workers should have run to the fence, but they didn't. When he saw what was happening, the criminal propelled his more-than-six-foot body off the running board and sprinted across the street toward the vacant lot. As he left the car, the package he carried fell from his arms, and ration books came pouring out. As he dashed toward the vacant lot I felt there was little hope of our catching him at the speed he was traveling.

But "sleeping" McIver, who was nearest to the suspect when he parked his car, chased him with a surprising burst of speed. The rest of us had no hope of catching him. As the suspect crossed the vacant lot McIver was only a couple of yards behind him, but was making no headway. I watched with amazement as the slim five-foot, eight inch, 140-pound McIver dived through the air and came within inches of grabbing his quarry. When in mid-air he must have realized he could not reach him in this way. He flipped over in an acrobatic somersault and thrust his legs forward, striking the suspect between the shoulder blades. They both crashed to the ground, with McIver on top of the suspect. As we looked around we saw that the suspect would not have had to jump the fence if he had reached it. In the corner to which he was running, he could have squeezed through a hole in the fence where a board was missing.

By the time of the arrest the informant had left the scene. We picked up the scattered ration books, and found more in the suspect's car. We charged him with being in possession of stolen property, for which a magistrate imposed a six-month jail term. Even today, many years after the incident, I am still amazed that the slim, boyish McIver, who barely reached the height requirements of the RCMP, should have saved the day for the Toronto black market squad.

SEVENTEEN

Police are accustomed to dealing with informants, some law abiding, some not. Some give information because they want to "play policeman", by working undercover with or without pay. Others give information for such reasons as patriotism, self-interest, or even spite. Many informants give information only to a particular policeman, who will not reveal their identity to anyone, including his superiors. Even I never knew the identity of the informant who got my name from a newspaper, and who continued to telephone me, periodically, for about two years on matters related to abuses of the gasoline rationing regulations.

One of my most interesting black market cases developed through an informant who would give information only to the officer in charge of the Criminal Investigation Branch (CIB), Inspector Bill Schutz. One morning in midsummer, 1944, Schutz called me to his office. He had received a visit that morning from a man who throughout the war had given him information on people of East-European origin whom he considered subversive. The man, whose previous information had not always been accurate, seemed to enjoy being involved in cloak-and-dagger operations. If Inspector Schutz was not available when he had information to give, he would give it only to the O.C. of the division, a superintendent, and never to anyone of lower rank. This time, however, due to the nature of his information he had agreed to deal with me, a lowly detective sergeant.

The inspector described the informant as Bulgarian, short and fat, with dark heavy eyebrows, a swarthy complexion and a heavy accent. He sounded to me like a character in a spy novel. His information concerned Adjutor Brulotte, who operated a bottle exchange in Quebec City, and who had recently visited him. Brulotte had mentioned that if ever the informant wanted some gasoline coupons, he simply had to ask for them. Brulotte knew of an unlimited supply.

Accompanied by Constable Barry Graham, I went to the informant's place of business, a small factory on Danforth Avenue, where he renewed old felt hats for the millinery trade. We saw at once that the inspector's description fitted him to a "T". He told us that when Brulotte offered him ration coupons he had not thought much about it. After thinking it over, however, he decided to report the matter to his friend, Inspector Schutz.

I suggested to the informant that he write to Brulotte, asking for some coupons and offering to pay for them. I thought he might refuse to get involved, leaving me to send his information to the RCMP in Quebec City. But he agreed, and insisted that I remain with him while he typed the letter to Brulotte.

A couple of weeks later, when I began to believe the informant had changed his mind about cooperating with the police, he telephoned me to say that he had received a shipment from Quebec City. He seemed very excited, and asked me to go immediately to his factory. It made me think that a shipment meant more than a few loose coupons. I entered the factory door and found the informant standing inside, waiting for me. He pointed to a package, about a cubic foot in size, on the floor. He stressed that that was the exact spot where the expressman had left the package, and that no one else had touched it. He called on a woman at work on a nearby sewing machine to confirm what he said. None of this was necessary, but it was in keeping with his cloak-and-dagger complex.

I took the package to his small office. While he watched I counted out an amazing 500 counterfeit gasoline ration books of category AA. Obviously Brulotte had access to a huge source, not merely of ration coupons but of counterfeit gasoline ration books. I could see that the printer must have had good counterfeit plates to achieve the excellent clarity of the printing. But the orange-coloured paper, not quite the orange of the genuine coupons, was easily discernible as counterfeit.

"Why do you think Brulotte sent you so many ration books?" I asked the informant.

"Perhaps he thought I might want to start a little business in counterfeit coupons," he answered, "so he sent what he considered a start-up supply." I wouldn't have been surprised if the informant had agreed to do so, and then had changed his mind.

It seemed that I had embarked on a gasoline ration coupon case of commercial proportions. I asked the informant if he would introduce me to Brulotte as a prospective buyer of ration books, although I anticipated that he might feel this was getting in too deep, and would refuse. To my surprise he agreed to do as I asked, and offered to telephone Brulotte immediately.

Then, as if he might be overheard, he lowered his voice. "What name are you going to use?" he whispered.

"My own," I answered, to his obvious disappointment.

He picked up the telephone and arranged with Brulotte for me to meet him in Quebec City in about a week.

In spite of my involvement to that point, I knew that because Quebec City was in the RCMP's "C" Division, with headquarters in Montreal, further investigation must be carried out by members of that division. But I also knew that my introduction to Brulotte, as a prospective buyer of his counterfeit ration books, would play an important part in their efforts to conclude the matter successfully. I notified Inspector Schutz of the arrangements, and he telephoned the C.O. of "C" Division. Schutz gave him the details of the situation, and notified him that I would take the counterfeit ration books to Montreal, to be guided by him as to further police action.

During the week before I was due in Montreal, I planned how best to deal with Brulotte. I decided to point out that the paper of his ration books was obviously counterfeit, and that it would easily be detected by the police. I would offer, if he were in any way involved with the printer, to get him a supply of genuine paper. I discussed this idea with a high official of the Oil Controller's office in Toronto, and he agreed that if the paper was necessary to further the investigation, he would make it available. Next I spent a couple of hours at Rolph, Clark Stone, taking a short course in the printing of genuine coupons. When I told the supervisor that I might need some paper in Quebec City, he assured me that he had plenty of 500-pound rolls in the warehouse.

During that week the informant telephoned me. True to his cloak-and-dagger character, he wanted to make sure, he said, that Brulotte would have no doubt that I was the person he had recommended. To ensure this he had a plan related to Brulotte's visit to Toronto several weeks before. He and Brulotte had gone to the Alexandra Theatre to see *The Old Soak,* played by W.C. Fields.

"I'll write a letter telling Brulotte that when he first meets you in Quebec City, he must ask you the name of the play he and I attended.

I'll tell him you will answer, *The Old Soak*. As no one else knows we went to the play, Brulotte will be sure you're the right man."

I didn't think we needed any code as a precaution, but if it made the informant happy I was agreeable. Obviously, if no cloak-and-dagger element was involved, the informant was going to supply it.

On arriving in Montreal with the package of ration books, I discussed the case with Sergeant Ted Chamberlain, who was in charge of the black market work in "C" division. He agreed that he would take over the investigation, and that I should continue my undercover contact with Brulotte. Our main job, we agreed, was to find the printer of the ration books, and the counterfeit printing plates that he used. To that time no policeman in Canada had been able to do such a thing, in spite of the many different types of counterfeit ration coupons then in circulation.

With Chamberlain and two of his men I drove to Quebec City, where we quickly installed ourselves on the seventh floor of the *Chateau Frontenac* hotel. We took three adjoining rooms, mine in the middle, the two constables on one side, and Chamberlain on the other. Immediately we "bugged" my room and linked it to listening devices in each of the other two. Then I was ready to receive Mr. Adjutor Brulotte.

I checked the telephone number the informant had given me with the bottle exchange number in the telephone book. Finding they were identical, I called Brulotte. When I said I would like to see him at his convenience, he promised to be "right over". Within minutes there was a knock on the door of my room. In walked a heavily built, middle-aged man, well dressed and with a jovial manner.

"I can supply all the coupons you want, in book or sheet form," he said with a laugh as soon as we had shaken hands. "For a price of course," he continued. "Printing coupons is not cheap nowadays."

Knowing that the men in the adjoining rooms were operating their listening devices and taking notes, I let him talk on. There was no doubt that he accepted me as the person the informant had mentioned to him, but I reminded him of the little scene we were to engage in.

"You are supposed to ask me, Mr. Brulotte, the name of the play you attended when you were in Toronto."

"Ah, yes," he laughed. *The Old Soak*, eh?"

So much for cloak-and-dagger codes.

Although Brulotte was ready to deal for any number of ration books that I wanted, the police needed time to be able to find out with whom Brulotte was associating, especially the printer. I told him I had no intention of buying the poor-quality ration books he was making, and I produced one of the books from his Toronto shipment as an example.

"If I tried to dispose of such books in Toronto," I scoffed, "I'd soon land in jail."

Using a police gasoline ration book for comparison, I pointed out the difference between the paper in his book and the paper in the genuine one. Brulotte was disappointed that he was not going to make an immediate deal, but he could easily see the difference in the quality of the papers. I didn't need any of the technical knowledge I had gained at Rolph, Clark Stone to prove my point.

"I should know about paper," I said, "I have worked in Rolph, Clark Stone's plant for fifteen years."

"If you aren't going to buy my books, what kind of deal are you ready to make?" Brulotte asked.

"I have a supply of the genuine paper, stolen from the plant in which I work, and stored in a secret warehouse," I responded. "I'll trade you a 500-pound roll of genuine paper for 100,000 AA category ration books. You'll have enough paper left over to print a lot more for yourself – on genuine paper, don't forget. I'll sell my books for ten dollars each, for a total of a million dollars." It was easy to talk big money under the circumstances.

"I'm not in this scheme alone," Brulotte said. "I'll have to discuss this with my partners. I'll let you know what they say later today."

"If they agree," I said, "I can get the paper sent here within three or four days by CN Express."

Before Brulotte left my room, he told me that I had arrived in Quebec City in the middle of a provincial election campaign. The election had been called by the Liberal government of Premier Godbout. Brulotte was a constituency organizer for Godbout's opponent, Maurice Duplessis, of the Union Nationale Party. Brulotte's constituency was L'Islet, some miles east of Quebec City, but near enough for him to drive there and back almost every day. Between running his business, and his visits to the constituency, he was a busy man, he stressed.

"If you're so busy with these other things, how come you're also involved in printing ration books?" I asked.

"It's connected with the election," he answered. "We organizers want to give a gasoline ration book and a bottle of homebrew to every voter in our constituencies."

Soon he left me, promising to return later in the day. He did so that evening.

"My partners can't go for the 100,000 book deal," he said. "The most they will go for is 35,000."

Frowning, I responded that I had no authority to agree to that low number. I must consult my partners in Toronto. I would talk to them by telephone later that night, and then I would give him a call at home. Of course I had no partners.

Later that night I telephoned Brulotte as agreed. I told him my partners could not agree to less than 75,000 books. He said he would put it up to his partners the next morning.

Meanwhile, Chamberlain's men and local RCMP members had planned to tail Brulotte each time he left the hotel. Our arrangement was that any time he and I stopped talking about our deal, and he was ready to leave my room, it was up to me to delay him by asking how the election campaign was progressing. This was a signal to the men in the other rooms, to hurry down to the hotel's front entrance, to be ready to follow him to his destination. After the first time or two, I used to accompany him down in the elevator to delay him as much as possible. When I hadn't been able to delay him long enough in the room, we often had company in the elevator – the members of the Force who were going to tail him.

We hoped Brulotte would lead them to where he was meeting his associates. His wild driving, however, made it impossible for the constables to follow him without giving themselves away. On leaving the hotel, he drove at such breakneck speeds, down the steep winding hill to Lowertown, that usually they soon lost him. On the few occasions they did manage to follow him down the hill, they soon lost him because he ignored red lights.

The day after I had made the 75,000 book offer, Brulotte came to my hotel room, notably less exuberant than when we first met.

"50,000 books is the absolute limit they'll go for," he said dejectedly. "They might have gone for more, but they have to print large numbers of ration books for themselves to give to the voters."

I knew that "my partners" were going to accept this latest offer, and I could have given him an answer immediately. But I didn't want to do so too readily.

"I'll have to get back to my partners in Toronto," I stalled. "I doubt if they'll go for only 50,000 books."

It took two days for "my partners" to agree to accept his second proposal.

It was now up to me to get the genuine paper to Quebec City. I telephoned the Oil Controller's office in Toronto, and spoke to the official who had promised to let me have the paper if I needed it. He agree to ship a 500-pound roll by way of the CN Express office. I thought the size of the roll might work to our advantage, since moving it from the express office to where the printer wanted it would enable us to follow it, hopefully to the print shop where the ration books were produced. When the paper arrived at the express office a few days later, however, things didn't work out the way I had hoped.

EIGHTEEN

I had been in Quebec City about ten days when the genuine gasoline ration paper arrived at the CN Express office. I had hoped Brulotte would have it delivered immediately to wherever the books were to be printed. If so, we could probably bring the case to an end by arresting those involved, retrieving the paper and, above all, finding the counterfeit plates used by the printer. But Brulotte said he had no place to keep the 500-pound roll and wanted only an amount he could deliver himself, about seventy-five pounds.

Although this was disappointing, I asked at the express office if I could leave the roll there and take possession of it in small lots. The express man agreed. As I thought it over, it seemed this might work in our favour. If Brulotte had taken the whole roll he might have stored it in his roomy bottle exchange, and delivered parts of it to the printer as required, without our knowledge. Now I would have to approve of any release before he could get more paper from the express office, and we would have more opportunities to follow him to his destination. As it was, when he took the first seventy-five pounds of paper, his typical reckless driving prevented us from following him.

Brulotte told me a few days later, "The printer has started printing your ration books."

Then began a series of excuses as to why the printer could not finish the job. The printer became ill; there was a death in his family; the printing machine had broken down. Another delay came when the machine really had broken down, and the printer had to wait for a part from Toronto. Even after the machine had been repaired, there was still some delay. The delays caused a suspension of operations for about two weeks. I remained in Quebec City. I was in touch with Brulotte daily, trying to find out how things stood and, of course, to hurry things along if at all possible.

One morning Brulotte came to my hotel room to make more excuses. With pretended heat I accused him of using my paper to print ration books for his voters in L'Islet.

"You don't give a damn about my books." I said.

"No, no, no!" he replied. "The printer is doing his best to print your books. You should be aware," he continued soothingly, "that filling your order is a big job."

"Maybe," I snapped, "but I have no proof that you have even begun to print ration coupons."

By this time Brulotte had difficulty controlling his temper.

"If you want proof, I'll bring you a sample of the coupons right after lunch," he shouted as he prepared to leave.

As prearranged with my colleagues, I began to talk politics. The listeners on each side of my room left their rooms to get to the hotel lobby before Brulotte, to be ready to follow him when he left the hotel. To delay him as much as possible, I left the room with him, continuing to question him about the political situation. When we arrived at the elevator, however, I found my colleagues waiting for it. This created a slight problem because they had difficulty getting to their cars in time to follow Brulotte. Nevertheless they managed to reach their cars before Brulotte and I emerged from the hotel. As usual he drove away at great speed. I jumped into a second police car, thinking that surely this time he would lead us to the printing plant.

Luck was with us. Heavy traffic and favourable traffic lights enabled us to follow him to St. Joseph Street in Lowertown. We saw him park his car, cross the street, and go into a fenced yard. One of the RCMP members in my car said there was a print shop in the yard. At last I thought Brulotte had led us to the printer of the coupons. He had done so but it was a long time before we were sure of it.

As we discussed our next move we saw Brulotte and a man in work clothes come out to the street. They crossed to Brulotte's car, a Buick of recent vintage, and drove off. We followed them to the Grande Allee, a boulevard of fine houses, in one of which Duplesses' Union Nationale party had its headquarters. They entered the building and stayed for an hour and a half. I was keenly aware that Brulotte had an appointment with me "right after lunch". Where would he get the sample coupons that he had promised me? Did the man from the print shop have them with him when he entered Brulotte's car? Or were the coupons being printed at that moment in the basement of the Union Nationale club, where we knew there was some kind of printing press? After about one and a half hours Brulotte left the club alone, entered his car and headed in the direction of the *Chateau Frontenac* hotel. To get back to the hotel in time, the car I was in raced through a back road, skirting the Plains of Abraham. I had been in my room only a few minutes when there was a knock on the door.

As soon as Brulotte entered he drew a folded sheet of genuine gasoline ration paper about as large as a newspaper page from his inside coat pocket. He handed it to me.

I unfolded it and saw it was an uncut sheet of printed gasoline ration coupons of good quality.

"You must have an excellent set of printing plates," I said as I rubbed a finger over the print and smudged it.

"The ink is still wet," I said.

"Yes," he agreed. "It takes an hour to dry."

I had discussed the counterfeit printing plates with Brulotte on several occasions, to see if I could find out who had made them. But he always put me off by saying that he had nothing to do with that end of the business.

His casual answer about drying time gave me a shock. It meant that the printing had been done in the basement of the Union Nationale club, while he was there for an hour and a half. It also meant that if the ration books being printed for me were delivered before we had located the printing press elsewhere, we would have to search the club. The RCMP was a federal force. The federal government was Liberal and so was the provincial government, then trying to be re-elected. A search of the Union Nationale party headquarters would be looked upon as a federal attack on the provincial Opposition party, in order to help the Godbout Liberal party stay in power. If we found evidence of counterfeiting in the club, it would not be so bad. On the other hand, if we didn't, all hell would break loose. Perhaps it wouldn't be so bad if the provincial Liberals were returned to power. But if the Union Nationale won and we had successfully concluded our investigation, things might get politically "sticky". But that was not my problem.

By the RCMP simply doing its duty it could be embroiled in a battle between the two political parties, and thus be accused of being a political tool of the federal Liberal party.

After Brulotte left my hotel room, I discussed the matter with

Sergeant Chamberlain, who after all was in charge of the investigation. We decided it would be prudent to alert RCMP headquarters in Ottawa. On the basis of Brulotte's remarks about the ink on the coupons taking an hour to dry, a search of the Union Nationale club was more than a possibility before our investigation ended. I telephoned the Director of Criminal Investigation in Ottawa, my old C.O., Assistant Commissioner V.A.M. Kemp, and explained the situation.

"Don't do anything until I call you back," he said. He needn't have worried. As we waited for his call I had visions of telephone conversations between RCMP Commissioner S.T. Wood and the Minister of Justice, Mr. Ernest Lapointe, the minister in charge of the RCMP. When Kemp called back, he asked:

"Have you got the search warrant for the club?" I had to answer, "No". "We agree with your plan to search the club," he continued, "but make sure the search is absolutely necessary." This we intended to do.

I believed Brulotte was sorry about the repeated delays in providing my ration books. To make my life happier he had invited me to his home for supper, but I had declined. Then he had invited me to accompany him to the constituency of L'Islet to see how he carried out his political organizing, and to pass the time while I waited for the delays to be overcome. This invitation I also declined. Later on I was very thankful that I had declined both invitations.

The delay in delivering my ration books gave Chamberlain time to consider where he should apply for search warrants for the U.N. club and other places we would have to search. The local political situation made it difficult for us to find a politically trustworthy justice of the Peace, not only to issue the warrants but also to keep silent.

Eventually, we found one. He was a close relative of a member of the RCMP detachment. He was a staunch Liberal, and lived on a farm far out in the country.

We obtained search warrants for all the places we suspected might be involved, including Jobidon's Drive-UR-Self business in lower town. We had seen Brulotte visit these offices several times. We learned that Jobidon was also a Union Nationale organizer. We suspected that he, too, was involved in the printing of gasoline ration coupons, in order to give the voters in his constituency a gasoline ration book and a bottle of illicit spirits to have them vote for the Union Nationale candidate. We had also found that the man who had accompanied Brulotte to the Union Nationale club, the day Brulotte produced the printing sample, was indeed the printer who owned the print shop on St. Joseph Street.

By now our men had visited the shop several times, under one pretext or another. But they found no sign of any coupons being printed. I kept pestering Brulotte to finish printing my books. I said I had spent all my holiday period in Quebec City, and that my company would be looking for my return. I made him think that day by day I was getting more annoyed at the delay, which was at least partly true.

At last, after I had annoyed Brulotte even more, and after I had been in Quebec City nearly a month, Brulotte told me "they" were going to make an extra effort to finish printing my books, because the election date was approaching and the books needed for his voters must also be printed.

It had baffled all of us as to why we could not find the printing place. Brulotte seemed to have some connection with the printer on St. Joseph Street, but there was no activity at his shop to indicate the printing of ration books. We had men watching it and the Union Nationale club day and night. We thought they might be printing at night, but our watchers saw no activity at either the print shop or the Union Nationale club.

Then came the day when Brulotte asked me for more paper from the roll in the express office. He was followed, but led the watchers to his home in St. Foy, where he put his car in his garage and locked the door. Thwarted again.

I suspected that "they" had used some of the paper to print some ration books for themselves. When I accused Brulotte of this he denied it, saying that they had wasted some paper when getting ready to print. He promised to have 3,000 books ready for me soon. But I was concerned that he would deliver the books before we had some idea as to where they were being printed. It was one thing to get the books, but it was equally important that we find the counterfeit printing plates. Delivery of the books would result in our having to make searches, and if the plates were not found it meant that we had accomplished only part of what we had set out to do. We had yet to find out where the books were printed. Another point we had to consider was that "they" might be printing counterfeit books for their own purpose. We wanted to prevent such books from being circulated.

Two days after receiving the second supply of paper, Brulotte phoned me to say "they" were ready to start delivering books to me in small lots. This didn't matter to me, but I pretended that it did. The next day at noon he called again to say there would be a delivery about 2 p.m. at the hotel.

It had been arranged that a delivery of books, regardless of the number, would be the signal for Chamberlain and his men to put into effect the search of places for which we had warrants. We would not execute the search warrant on the Union Nationale club, however, until we were satisfied that it was necessary because of our lack of success in the other places. We had also decided that I should not take part in the searches, but that I should keep undercover until I gave evidence at the trial.

Brulotte telephoned me several times that afternoon, each time putting off the time of delivery by an hour or so. Each time we had to notify the search teams allocated to the various places. In any case, the team detailed to search the Union Nationale club must wait for a special messenger before beginning its search. Without such a messenger they were to take no action.

At last, about 7 p.m., after five hours of waiting, my telephone rang and a strange voice said, "Mr. Kelly, I have something down here for you. Can you come down?" meaning down to the hotel lobby.

Watched by several RCMP members, I met a young man about eighteen years of age waiting for me in the lobby. He led me to a four-door car parked at the front entrance. The back compartment was filled high with packages.

"How many books have you got?" I asked.

"Three thousand," he said.

I signaled to an RCMP member that the car contained ration books, and he went to signal the search parties. I thought I should take possession of the books on the spot, but the young man insisted that he must take me down to Jobidon's Drive-UR-Self offices in Lowertown, I never learned why, and he started to drive off.

We started down the hill beside the hotel, and I decided not to go to Jobidon's place.

"Stop the car," I ordered the young driver. He didn't understand and kept going. Rather than argue with him I took the key out of the ignition. He pulled to the side of the road. I identified myself and told him he was under arrest. I asked him his name and he said it was Jobidon.

The two police cars that had been following me sped by at a fast clip. Only the men in the second car noticed we had parked, and they returned to see what had happened. I told them to take the youth, the car, and the packages to their detachment.

By this time the other car had returned and I got into it. We went to Lowertown where the men in the car had been assigned to search Jobidon's place of business. They parked about a block away from Jobidon's, in a spot from which I could see the office. As a result of the decision that I should remain undercover, I sat in the car to await the result of their search. I had already broken my "cover" when I had arrested young Jobidon.

I had sat there about half an hour when I saw a man leave Jobidon's office. As he walked toward me, I recognized him as the man who had come out of the print shop with Brulotte, and had gone to the Union Nationale club the day I had received the sample of the printed ration coupons. I couldn't imagine why the searchers had allowed him to leave, unless perhaps they had not recognized him. As he came abreast of me I got out of the car and stopped him.

"Are you the printer from St. Joseph's Street?" I asked.

"I am," he replied.

I identified myself and took him back to the police car for questioning. Much to my surprise, and after only a little prodding, he admitted he was the printer who printed the ration books. But, he said, he printed them not in his printing shop, but in a garage in an alley around the corner from it.

I asked him to take me there. As I didn't have the key to the police car we walked several blocks to a row of one-car garages in the alley.

He stopped at one, unlocked the door and switched on the light. I was delighted to see a printing press, a large number of ration books already made up, sheets of uncut coupons, and sheets of paper cut to size for printing. Most important, the printing plates were in the press. I took possession of the plates. I told the printer he was under arrest, and that everything in the garage was under seizure. I took the plates with me.

I locked the garage door and we went to the police car. On the way he told me that he had done the printing at night, except for that day when he had worked all day to get a shipment ready. He did not know they were for me. He did not have to go near his print shop when he went to the garage. He simply left his home and went down the alley, without appearing on the street where his print shop was located.

Soon after we got to the car the searchers had finished at Jobidon's. They had found ample evidence that Jobidon was involved in the conspiracy. I told them what had occurred in their absence, and asked that someone advise Sergeant Chamberlain. Thus the search of the Union Nationale club would be called off, and the seized exhibits in the printer's garage collected. I handed the plates to them.

By late that night all the search warrants had been executed, and six persons arrested, including Adjutor Brulotte. At each place searched, evidence of the involvement in the conspiracy was found.

Also, each person arrested had counterfeit coupons in his possession, all printed on genuine paper.

I thought it prudent to call the Director of Criminal Investigation in Ottawa, to tell him what had happened, and what had not happened – a search of the Union Nationale club.

It amused me that we had search warrants for many places, even one that was unnecessary, but that most of the evidence was found in a place, the garage, for which we had no warrant.

The next morning the news of our operation pushed the war off the front pages of the Quebec City newspapers, both French and English. Much was made of the fact that two of those arrested were organizers for the Union Nationale party. No doubt the provincial Liberals read these stories with great glee. The arrested men had appeared before a magistrate, and had been granted bail.

The preliminary hearing would not be held for some time, so I returned to Toronto, leaving Sergeant Ted Chamberlain and his men, who had all the evidence, to prepare the case for the prosecution. Before leaving Quebec City, I left instructions for the remainder of the Oil Controller's paper to be shipped back to Toronto.

I went back to Montreal by police car, and from there by train to Toronto. As I sat in the train my mind went back a couple years to the night I guarded the police cars near Cooksville, west of Toronto, while others had gone to a railroad switch which had been tampered with in an attempt to derail the Chicago Flyer. One of the constables with me had suggested that while we waited we should search for tracks in the snowy fields nearby.

This resulted in our finding the culprit, while those at the switch had found no clue to lead them to anyone who might have committed the offence. Now, in Quebec City, I had been sitting in a car just waiting for members of the RCMP to complete a search when the printer came along and took me to the evidence we had been hoping for since I had arrived in Quebec City, about a month earlier.

If it had not been for this fortuitous incident, although we had enough evidence to convict those arrested, we might not have put the printer out of his illegal business.

From what I had heard about Quebec politics and politicians in Quebec City, it led me to hope fervently, for the sake of our prosecution, that Godbout's Liberals would be returned to power at the forthcoming election. I was not partial to that or any other political party. But I had learned that if the accused at the forthcoming preliminary hearings were committed for trial in a higher court, the prosecutor would be appointed by the provincial Attorney General. I dreaded a trial in which the prosecutor had been appointed by a newly elected

Duplessis government to prosecute his election workers. After all, they wanted the counterfeit ration books to encourage voters to help elect the Duplessis government.

The morning after I returned home, I telephoned the informant to tell him what had happened. He had wondered what was happening, he said, until he had heard the news on the radio. He presumed that what had happened was the result of the information he had given the RCMP. I assured him that it was. I didn't tell him that his "Old Soak" identification code hadn't worked.

About two weeks after the arrests Duplessis's Union Nationale party was elected.

NINETEEN

Although the Quebec City investigation had ended early in July, the preliminary hearing, held before County Court Judge Fortier, did not begin until about three months later. I found it strange that a County Court judge was to preside. In English Canada I had seen only magistrates and Justices of the Peace act in that capacity. I was told that in Quebec some judges customarily acted as magistrates. The judge was an unusually mild-mannered, elderly man. I thought that perhaps because of the politics involved in the case, he had been especially chosen so that defence counsel could browbeat him. Later, the antics of the defence counsel in court seemed to confirm my suspicions, but this in no way affected the decisions he made. The six accused were charged with various offences under the Oil Controller's regulations, including a charge of conspiracy. As this was a preliminary hearing they did not have to plead guilty or not guilty. They were defended by Messrs Flynn and Blais, two lawyers known for their connections with the Union Nationale party, the government of the province since the election about two months earlier. Mr. Maurice Boisvert was the federal Liberal government's appointed prosecutor.

When the preliminary hearings began, they created considerable public interest, and the courtroom was filled to capacity. I was the first witness to testify, and gave my evidence through an interpreter. Although defence counsel didn't interfere with my giving evidence, they seemed intent on disturbing the atmosphere of the proceedings. On several occasions Flynn objected to the interpretation of what I had said. As all concerned spoke English very well, they undoubtedly knew what I had said. It so happened that the interpreter was invariably right, but the interruption usually seemed to suit defence purposes. At other times both Flynn and Blais made loud laughing remarks to each other. They showed no respect for the judge, and paid little attention to his requests to refrain from such behaviour.

My evidence had consisted of how I had arrived in Quebec City to make a deal with Brulotte for counterfeit ration books. I described the deal in detail, and my long wait for the books to be printed. I described the delivery of the books at the *Chateau Frontenac* hotel, and the arrest of the printer when he took me to the garage in which the printing was taking place. In dealing with Brulotte, I said, I had used my own name, that I had pretended to be a salesman for Rolph, Clark Stone, the company that printed all the genuine gasoline coupons for use throughout Canada. I presented as an exhibit the counterfeit plates I had found in the garage. There was much more, but this was the main part of my evidence.

As the hearing continued, Flynn and Blais continued to make loud comments to each other. When Flynn began to cross-examine me he asked, "Are you a Mason?" I answered, "Yes." Both defence counsel immediately sprang to their feet to object to my giving evidence. Flynn said that as a Mason I didn't believe in God, and therefore could not give evidence in a Quebec court. Although the judge tried to bring some order to the proceedings, it seemed that defence counsel had total control. The seemingly bewildered judge appeared to have little control or authority. Prosecutor Boisvert, rather bemused, watched the proceedings from his table. He occasionally rose to object to the behaviour of defence counsel, but was unable to speak above the din they created. He threw up his hands as Flynn and Blais, laughing hilariously, continued to shout at the judge.

I stood in the witness box watching it all, scarcely able to believe I was in a Canadian court. I had given evidence in many Canadian courts, but had never seen behaviour even remotely approaching this. Whether it was defence counsel's euphoria after the election of their party as the provincial government, or a means of making it impossible for the judge to continue with the hearing, I couldn't say. In any case, the behaviour of defence counsel was making it impossible for the hearing to continue in an orderly manner.

Their jocular remarks, made in French, which I could not understand, delighted both the accused and the spectators. The court rocked with laughter. Eventually the judge brought some semblance of order, but it was obviously impossible to continue with the hearing. He adjourned the proceedings after saying, first in French, and then in English for my benefit, that he would study the defence objection to my giving evidence, and would give his decision the following morning. Messrs Flynn and Blais collected their papers and boisterously left the room. Mr. Boisvert told me he had never seen such an exhibition in any courtroom he had attended.

The next morning the courtroom was unable to hold all those who had come to enjoy the second episode of the judicial circus in Judge Fortier's court. I returned to the witness box and the very dignified judge asked me if I belonged to the English Rite of the Masonic Order. I said no, but that the lodge I had belonged to operated under the Scottish Rite, which was practically the same thing.

"If you are a member of either Rite," he said to me in English, "I will believe every word you say." He did not qualify his decision, but I understood him to mean he would believe me only if I told the truth.

Mr. Flynn, indicating that he was unhappy with the decision, got up to continue his examination of me.

"Are you married?" he asked.

"Yes," I said.

"Have you any children?"

"No," I answered.

Flynn shrugged his shoulders and threw up his hands, while he and Blais laughingly made remarks to each other. Mr. Boisvert objected to Flynn's line of questioning. The Judge chastised both defence lawyers. But it made no difference. It seemed they had not come to court to defend their clients, but to make a farce of the proceedings. In this they were succeeding extremely well. Flynn questioned me again and again, about what I had said during my original evidence. He found it difficult to ask a question to which the answer did not reflect on his clients' guilt. He seemed to have no plan of attack, except to keep asking questions, seemingly oblivious of the adverse effect of my answers on the accused. As we expected, he attacked the manner in which the RCMP had conducted the investigation, the way we had led Brulotte into our "net", and the way I had led him to believe I was an employee of Rolph, Clark Stone.

The defence knew nothing of the notes members of the RCMP had taken of the conversations between Brulotte and myself in my hotel room, about which Chamberlain and his men would give evidence later. But before I left the witness box I was forced to reveal that fact.

As his cross-examination was about to end, Mr. Flynn switched his line of questioning and asked if I could recall a particular day in

July. I said I couldn't, but I might refresh my memory if I referred to my notebook.

"I don't think that what I have in mind is the subject for note taking," he said.

After whispering to Blais he asked, "Do you remember receiving a visit from a blonde lady the afternoon of the date I mentioned?"

I knew immediately he was trying to attack my character.

"I did not entertain a blonde lady in my room that afternoon nor at any other time," I answered. I wondered if I should then reveal that all conversations in my room had been recorded. I concluded that there was no better way to put a stop to such questioning. I told Flynn that whatever visits I received, such as those from Adjutor Brulotte, could be checked by the records kept by members of the RCMP who were listening in the adjoining rooms.

My answers took Flynn and Blais by surprise. As if he had never asked the question about the blonde lady Flynn returned to his aimless questioning. Nevertheless, everyone knew the purpose of his introducing the blonde Lady. If I hadn't any evidence to support my denial, he would have produced a blonde lady to give whatever evidence he wanted her to give. It would certainly have harmed my credibility, as Flynn intended. I was thankful I had refused Brulotte's invitations to his home for dinner, and to the constituency of L'Islet when he went there to carry out his duties as a Union Nationale organizer. What a story they could have concocted about my behaviour on such visits.

During my cross-examination, a slight commotion was caused by the entry of two men who had been seated with great deference at the defence table. I learned later that both were high-level politicians in the Duplessis government, one of them the newly appointed Attorney General. If anything more were needed to emphasize the political overtones of the hearing, the presence of the Attorney General at the defence table provided it. It indicated to the accused that they had the support of the politicians they had helped to elect. It was also a blatant attempt to intimidate the judge.

The next witness was Sergeant Ted Chamberlain who spoke impeccable French. He didn't seem to be surprised at the behaviour of defence counsel. He had long experience in Quebec courts, and now he knew Flynn had no more pertinent questions than those he had asked of me. I judged Chamberlain to be the kind of person who could give as much as he could take, and perhaps a little more.

"Are you a Mason? Flynn asked.

I had no idea that he was, but was not surprised when he said he was one. Flynn raised the same objections as he had done with me. As a Mason, Chamberlain could not believe in God, and therefore could not give evidence in a Quebec court. The judge had heard it all before and immediately overruled Flynn. I was surprised at his next question.

"Are you a Catholic?" he asked.

"Yes," said Chamberlain without hesitation. Then followed considerable bickering between Chamberlain and Flynn, about his being both a Mason and a Catholic. At last Chamberlain ended the exchange.

"I am an Anglo-Catholic," he stated. "I was raised in the Anglican church."

Chamberlain's Irish wit and his fluency in French had enabled him to deal adequately with Flynn.

Chamberlain's cross-examination was interrupted when Blais rose to complain vehemently about the RCMP searching the home of the accused, Brulotte, that morning, and seizing a typewriter. The RCMP had done this because we believed that it was the typewriter Brulotte had used to write the letter which my informant had received in Toronto, in which mention was made of supplying him with coupons.

Both defence counsel waved their arms and shouted at the judge. The circus had returned. They claimed the police had acted improperly, and had shown great disrespect for the court. These tongue-in-cheek remarks evoked laughter from the onlookers.

Eventually Flynn and Blais allowed the judge to speak. He declared that the police had a responsibility to search for evidence wherever and whenever they might reasonably expect to find any. They had not been disrespectful to the court in doing so, as alleged by defence counsel.

As the judge concluded his remarks, Flynn and Blais, who only a few minutes earlier had criticized the police for some imagined disrespect for the court, picked up their papers, and without saying a word they strode from the court.

The judge adjourned the hearing. It re-opened after lunch, when defence counsel returned without apologizing. Such behaviour would not have been countenanced in an Ontario court. Perhaps Judge Fortier was intimidated to some degree, knowing that the accused and defence counsel were closely connected to the newly elected provincial government.

I was sure that the visit of the newly appointed Attorney General to the defence counsel's table had not gone unobserved. In Ontario, far less improper behaviour than that of Flynn and Blais would have resulted in disciplinary action by the law society.

By now I had a great respect for Judge Fortier. Despite the disruptions by defence counsel, the quiet-spoken judge always made the right decisions. Even so, he could do nothing to prevent Flynn and Blais making loud remarks about the prosecution being nothing more than a federal, Liberal, Protestant plot against Quebecers. If anything needed to be said about the unseemly behaviour of defence counsel, the special prosecutor, Mr. Boisvert, provided it.

"They know the evidence against them is overwhelming. They have nothing to lose by making a circus out of the hearings."

The fact that the RCMP were prosecuting Quebecers, for wartime offences, did nothing to enhance its popularity in the province of Quebec. For some months before, the RCMP had been roughly criticized for shooting a draft dodger during his attempt to escape. It resulted in two RCMP members being charged with murder. At the time of our preliminary hearings, they were being tried in the high court sitting in the same building. A ruling of the Supreme Court of Canada set them free.

After Chamberlain had given evidence, our cases were adjourned for a week. I returned to Toronto where I learned that the Toronto *Telegram* had covered my cross-examination by Flynn about being a Mason. It headlined one issue, "Masons Do Not Believe in God". It resulted in my receiving a number of requests to visit Masonic lodges to tell my story. But I declined each one.

I returned to Quebec City on two further occasions, to attend the continuing preliminary hearings. But it was clear that Flynn and Blais were interested only in delaying the hearings as much as possible. After several further adjournments, the judge committed all six accused for trial in a higher court. On the basis of the evidence, Judge Fortier could hardly have done anything else. Because of the heavy political overtones, however, I would not have been surprised if for some reason the charges had been dismissed.

I waited to be called back to Quebec City for the trial. But I was never called back. I received word from the RCMP in Montreal that the accused had pleaded guilty to some of the charges. The main characters, including Brulotte and Jobidon, had been fined $1000, and their helpers were fined lower amounts. It seemed very clear to me that such light punishment, for very serious offences, could only have come about as the result of political pressure. In an Ontario court at that time, persons convicted of such offences would have drawn two or more years in the penitentiary.

I had always believed that law enforcement and politics did not mix. Now I could prove it. But still, I was surprised to learn that even in Quebec such activity could be so bare faced.

TWENTY

Although experts had worked on each year's ration books to make them more difficult to counterfeit, counterfeiters always produced commendable likeness early in the rationing year. Gasoline rationing ended in the spring of 1945, shortly before the end of World War II in Europe. However, the new ration books had already been issued. Within days counterfeit 1945 gasoline ration books appeared on the street. The 1945 counterfeit ration books were so good that ordinary citizens could not tell the difference between the genuine and counterfeit coupons. They were also the earliest of any year on the black market.

Fortunately, we did not have to concern ourselves with them very long. We derived some satisfaction from knowing that the skills of the counterfeiters, and the cost of producing their products, would bring them little or no profits.

Although the enforcement of the gasoline rationing regulations had taken up most of the black markets squad's time, the end of gasoline rationing did not mean that we would have less work to do. There still remained a number of prosecutions which had begun, and many other wartime regulations to be enforced.

Because of our concern with numerous other regulations, we had left the matter of price ceiling infractions, except those involving used cars, to the civilian inspectors of the Wartime Prices and Trade Board. These inspectors, all of whom were civilians without any enforcement experience, did not enforce the regulations with any vigor.

They dealt only with complaints they received, and even then, if there was the slightest difficulty, they called upon the RCMP for assistance. The question facing us now was – where do we start?

We knew that abuses of the price ceiling regulations were widespread. Now, with manpower to spare, I looked around to see where the black market squad could be the most productive.

Our attention was drawn to price ceiling abuses in the men's clothing industry. Constable Kirkman of the black market squad wanted to buy a suit. He went to a well-known tailor on Queen Street west. He had decided on a suit when the tailor told him that in addition to the price ceiling quoted, he would have to pay an additional sum.

"Why should I pay extra?" Kirkman asked.

"Because I have to pay extra when I buy the cloth from the wholesaler."

Kirkman left without buying a suit, and went to a second tailor shop. The story there was the same. He related his experience when he returned to the office, and it became the basis for an investigation into the retail and wholesale men's clothing business.

Members of the black market squad went to several tailor shops and pretended to want to buy a suit. In each case the tailor demanded an extra amount of money over the ceiling price, because he had to pay extra to the wholesaler. We considered proceeding by the test purchase method, purchasing a suit in each case. But that procedure would have been too lengthy, and perhaps unnecessary. Instead, we seized each tailor's records, to find out as much as possible from them.

We had seized so many records, from ten tailors, that we had to use an office to store them. A member of the black market squad was always in attendance to supervise the tailors when they came to check their seized records, in order to carry out their daily business. In most cases we had seized not only the normal records, but also second sets of records that showed secret payments to a cloth wholesaler on Spadina Avenue. These secret records corresponded to the normal records, but only showed the extra amounts that had been paid. The normal records showed purchases at the price ceiling, whereas the secret records listed the yardage purchased and amount paid in addition to the price ceiling. For example: Date, 50 yards – $50. Invariably we found that the tailors paid one dollar a yard over the ceiling price.

These secondary records were not kept in formal account books, but on sheets of paper and in small notebooks we had found in the tailors' desk drawers. As well as being of interest to the black market squad, we believed that the federal Income Tax department would be very interested in these records, and those of the wholesaler from whom the tailors had purchased the cloth, whose records we intended to seize.

All the purchases of the tailors from whom we had seized records were made at the same wholesale firm – Shiffer-Lightman on Spadina Avenue. Our ample evidence allowed us to obtain a search warrant, and seize that company's records. In the case of each of the ten tailors, we had been able to haul the seized records to our office in a police car. In the case of Shiffer-Lightman, however, we needed a truck, and when this seizure arrived, we had to move all the exhibits to a larger office.

When we notified the Income Tax department, they showed keen interest in the records we had seized, and sent two accountants to work on them. We had found enough evidence on our own to prosecute the tailors and Shiffer-Lightman. But it was comforting to know that if the tax accountants found any additional information, we, too, could make use of it. But after a couple of days working on the Shiffer-Lightman books, the accountants could find no evidence of the company receiving any money over the ceiling price for the cloth it had sold to the ten tailors.

The tax accountants, however, were quite happy. They found enough evidence to show that the company, and Shiffer and his son, had avoided paying their full income tax for several years. Also, they had enough evidence from the seized tailors' books to show that Shiffer-Lightman had received money for sales that had not been recorded.

The tax accountants, like most civilian government investigators, seemed to have little interest in a prosecution for whatever offences they uncovered. In fairness to them, however, they knew that invariably income tax prosecutions resulted in nominal penalties, because the courts were aware that the payment of back taxes and the resultant penalties would amount to substantial amounts. I could confirm that the courts seemed unusually lenient with persons charged under the Income Tax Act. I had listened to a number of income tax cases in magistrate's court. I had found it somewhat ironic to hear defence counsel plead for a light sentence from the magistrates, because of the heavy taxes and penalties that had been assessed by the Income Tax department. All too often these pleas found sympathetic ears.

The records of Shiffer-Lightman revealed other tailors who had paid above ceiling prices for cloth. With the evidence of the tailors, and the records, we had ample evidence on which to base charges of price ceiling infractions against them. We wondered why, by searching all their records, we had not been able to find any record of overpayments to the company.

One day the elderly Mr. Shiffer came to look at his records. He complained bitterly that having to walk up two long flights of stairs was bad for his ailing heart. After checking his records in the exhibit room, he came to my office to ask when he could get his records back.

"As soon as the accountants are through with them," I answered.

Because of his heart condition, I reached for a chair so that he could sit down. As he bent forward to sit, two small black books fell from his vest pocket. With the vigor of a young man he bent to pick them up. But I had learned a lot about little black books, and I quickly stepped on them. I pushed him back into his chair and picked them up.

The elderly man, who had complained about a heart ailment, lunged at me with surprising ferocity. He tried to snatch the little blacks books from my hand, and began to wrestle with me. Men in the outer office heard the commotion and rushed in to see what was happening. They seized Shiffer, sat him down in a chair, and held him there while I took a quick look through the books. In view of his violent attempt to retrieve them, I was not surprised to see that they contained the information we had been unable to find in his company's records or elsewhere.

The books contained the names of tailors, dates and yardage purchased, and the amount collected over the ceiling price – one dollar a yard – and total amounts. All we had to do was compare the records in his little black books with his regular records, and those of the tailors. Our case against him, his son and the company was complete. Not only did the little black books show his dealings with "our" tailors, but with others as well.

I explained to Mr. Shiffer that, as the books contained evidence, I was duty bound to keep them. He threatened to prosecute me for keeping them, but eventually he cooled down and left the building. After making a lengthy schedule, showing in detail Shiffer-Lightman's black market transactions, I turned the books over to the income tax accountants.

We charged the Shiffers, father and son, as well as the company, with a number of offences under the price ceiling regulations. They were all heavily fined, and the younger Shiffer received nine months in jail.

The elder Shiffer escaped a jail term when he produced a doctor who stated that he had a serious heart condition, although the fracas in my office indicated that it was not too serious. But jail or not was a matter for the court. When the case was over we estimated that between court fines, tax, and tax penalties, the Shiffers paid about $500,000 in all. The ten original tailors, and others named in Shiffer's black books, were all prosecuted and received substantial fines.

In October 1945 I became involved in a matter so secret that I didn't know the names of the persons involved. The officer in charge of RCMP Special Branch called me in one day, and said he wanted food ration books for four people, but he refused to give me their names. He merely said that I must believe the ration books would be used to obtain rationed goods for people living in Canada. I realized that something important must have taken place for such a curious request.

I told my story to the enforcement counsel of the Wartime Prices and Trade Board, signed for the books, and took them to the officer. In due course I learned that the ration books were for Igor Gouzenko, who had just defected from the Soviet Embassy in Ottawa, his wife and two children. They had been brought to the Toronto area for protection.

Some months later I was again connected with the Gouzenko case. Superintendent Schutz, recently promoted, told me to report to the RCMP Director of Criminal Investigation in Ottawa. He didn't know exactly why I was needed, but it had something to do with the Gouzenko case. In Ottawa I found two RCMP members who had come from Montreal. I learned from them that we were required to analyze documents seized during searches of the homes and offices of the men who were suspected Soviet spies as a result of the Gouzenko revelations. It was our job to see what evidence the documents contained. To show, if possible, their contact with each other, with anyone or anything connected with the Soviet Embassy, or anything that might show that a conspiracy to commit espionage existed. It was obvious that what we found would form the basis of interrogation of those detained, as well as evidence in any resultant prosecution.

In spite of the piles of documents in cartons, the job was extremely interesting because of the importance of linking spy suspects to one another, to known spies in the Soviet Embassy, and to other possible conspirators, then unsuspected.

Much later, charges were laid under the Official Secrets Act against a number of alleged spies. We three investigators who had analyzed the documents attended the trials in Ottawa for the purpose of proving continuity of the documents, and identifying those which were used as evidence.

I found it interesting that the first time I went to Ottawa to examine the seized documents, I slept in a barrack room, on the same floor in Rockcliffe barracks on which the spy suspects were being held. Their barrack room was guarded twenty-four hours a day, and ceiling lights were on night and day. Each suspect slept on the same kind of barrack bed as I did, and we all ate the same food, provided by the RCMP mess.

The news media made much ado about the suspects being detained without any charges against them, and being held incommunicado. Actually, the RCMP was following the advice of counsel who were preparing for a hearing before a Royal Commission. Superintendents M.F.E. Anthony and "Slim" Harvison, both with long, field police experience, interviewed the detainees, one at a time, in a nearby building then known as the Police College. They often based their questioning on the documents we extracted from those seized, after we had discussed the significance of such documents with them.

The detainees themselves never complained about their treatment by the police. But because of the publicity given their detention in the news media, Mr. Justice Kellock, the chairman of the Royal Commission, made special mention of it at the end of the hearings, and later in the official report.

Meanwhile, the black market squad continued its investigations in Toronto and other parts of southern Ontario, under the capable supervision of Constable (later Inspector) Barry Graham.

The Royal Commission on Espionage was authorized by the federal government on February 5, 1946. It submitted its final report in June 1946. The report stated that most of the suspects had communicated official secrets to a foreign power. There was no doubt in anyone's mind who that power was – the Soviet Union. The two most prominent persons named were Fred Rose, a Communist M.P. for a Montreal riding, and Sam Carr, whose proper name was Schmil Kogan, a well-known Communist who, as far back as 1931, was sentenced to five years in the penitentiary for being a member of an unlawful association. When the Labour-Progressive Party was formed during the war to replace the banned Communist Party, he became its national organizer. Both Rose and Carr were also named as recruiters for agents of the foreign power referred to.

Within a year of the establishing of the Royal Commission, eighteen persons, involved in the espionage activities, had been charged under the Official Secrets Act and had appeared in the criminal courts. Gouzenko testified at the trial of each of them, as did the

RCMP members involved in the investigation. The hearing of the cases and subsequent appeals lasted over a period of 32 months. In all, ten were convicted and sentenced to various terms of imprisonment, up to six years. Three others were charged with obtaining false passports, and Dr. Alan Nunn May was sentenced to ten years in jail by a court in London, England. A prominent scientist, named Fuchs, escaped prosecution by fleeing to his native Germany.

Warrants for Sam Carr and a woman named Freda Linton were outstanding until the end of 1948. When the FBI arrested Carr in New York City he was turned over to the RCMP. In April 1949 he was convicted and sentenced to six years in prison for conspiring with U.S.S.R. embassy officials to utter a forged passport for a Russian agent. Linton surrendered to the RCMP about the same time, but charges against her were withdrawn because of lack of evidence. Nine other persons named in the Royal Commission report were acquitted in the criminal courts.

Igor Gouzenko and his family became wards of the government, and he lived incognito for the rest of his life. He remained under the protection of the RCMP only as long as he allowed them to protect him. It reached the stage where he refused to take any advice from them. He appeared on television with a bag over his head, and moved about the Toronto area without any disguise at all. It was believed that the USSR had little interest in him after relations between Canada and the Soviet Union improved.

In later years, because of my position as the Director of Security and Intelligence, I became periodically involved with Gouzenko when he requested, through the RCMP, increases in the amount the government was paying him. This did not always result in his being satisfied, and he frequently wrote to the Prime Minister expounding his case.

Gouzenko believed that his service to Canada, in exposing the spy ring, was worth more than the government was willing to pay. It cannot be denied that his services in doing so had been considerable.

TWENTY-ONE

During the war years, men in the RCMP black market squad dealt with dozens of different police forces in western and southern Ontario. The ones we were in contact with most frequently were the Ontario Provincial Police and the police of the largest cities. Only once was there an unpleasant incident. It might have caused a great deal of friction on the working level, thus ending the fine cooperation that existed between the Toronto city police and ourselves. Whenever members of police forces came across anything that suggested an infraction of wartime regulations, they passed the information to the RCMP black market squad. They often worked with us until the case was completed, rather than prosecute the cases themselves. This worked well because very often the resultant investigation took RCMP investigators beyond the working jurisdiction of the city police. Also, I believed, that since the laws infringed were federal statutes, the city police felt that offences against wartime regulations should be handled by the federal force – the RCMP. Nevertheless, they were prepared to cooperate to the fullest extent.

This was particularly so with the Toronto City police. To repay them we would arrange to have our prisoners booked in at Divisional police stations in the name of city police officers who cooperated with us, whether they were actually involved in the case or not.

I found the men I dealt with to be fine, honourable men, but as in every organization there were some bad apples. One of them created an incident that could have resulted in the cooperation we enjoyed coming to an abrupt end.

A city detective had arrested a man for some offence, and when searching him found that he had 800 pages of genuine gasoline ration coupons, four coupons to a page. He was obviously a trafficker who had a supplier with access to a greater supply. We questioned him in an office on the second floor of No. 2 police station, at Dundas and Bay Streets.

We had earlier arrested a number of persons, working in factories in Toronto's west end, for gasoline coupon offences. Many had to do with counterfeit coupons, but in the aircraft plant where the arrested man worked, others had been found in possession of genuine coupons. We concluded that the arrested man was the supplier at this plant. Later we found this to be true.

When I questioned him in the presence of the city police detective, he seemed ready to tell us all we wanted to know. After he disclosed the names of other traffickers, members of the black market squad immediately searched their homes. In each case they found evidence of trafficking in coupons, and arrested the individuals involved. By suppertime we had arrested eight such traffickers, and had obtained from them information on other traffickers, including their supplier. The latter was an ex-employee of Rolph, Clark Stone, who printed the coupons for the government. He also had a contact in the firm of Hinde and Dauche, where the Oil Controller sent loose pages of coupons for destruction. We were sure that the prisoner had a lot more to tell us, and decided to continue our interrogation after supper.

I suggested that, instead of putting the prisoner back in the cell to have his supper, the city detective, RCMP Constable Jim Lumb, myself and the prisoner should go to a nearby restaurant. Then the four of us went to the washroom. The detective and I left first, and waited on the landing for Lumb and the prisoner. As we waited I saw a man, bleeding badly about the face, emerge from the washroom. I didn't recognize him. Then Jim Lumb appeared, and I saw that the bleeding man was our prisoner.

Lumb explained he had been standing at a urinal to the right of the prisoner. A city detective sergeant stood on the left. Without any warning, and for no apparent reason, the sergeant turned and struck the prisoner repeatedly. When Lumb intervened, the sergeant gave no excuse for what he had done. When the sergeant came out of the washroom I asked him why he had abused the prisoner; I got no more out of him than had Lumb. He was intoxicated.

From the state the prisoner was in, he could not come to supper with us, nor did he wish to do so. He was placed in the cell. We told the duty sergeant of the incident and asked that the prisoner be attended to, and a doctor called if necessary. It was clear that we could not continue our interrogation. As we put the prisoner in the cell, he wondered aloud if that was the payment for his cooperating with the police.

Early the next morning I reported the matter to RCMP Superintendent Schutz, and told him exactly what had happened. I told him that I was sure the detective sergeant would be charged with assault, and that Lumb and I would be called as witnesses. He wasn't a bit concerned. If that was the case, he said, let the chips fall where they may. He would take the matter up with Chief Draper of the city police, he said, so that he could take whatever internal action he deemed necessary. That was fine with me, because that was the way I wanted it. I not only felt strongly about prisoners being abused, but I was sure that the detective sergeant had prevented the prisoner from giving us a great deal more information. Nevertheless, I could see cooperation between the two forces diminishing when two members of the RCMP gave evidence in court against the detective sergeant.

The next morning in court, all the accused appeared, including the man with the beaten-up face. His lawyer asked the magistrate to take note of his condition, because he intended to refer to it later. The cases were adjourned for a week, and the accused were allowed their freedom on bail. All the cases were disposed of in a few weeks, except that of the man who had been beaten up by the detective sergeant. We were waiting for the city detective to give evidence on our behalf, but he kept putting off his appearance on some pretext or another. Obviously he was being kept away from court until the accused's face had healed sufficiently. Then, when there were only a few scars left on the man's face, the detective turned up and the case was disposed of, with the accused receiving a jail term. No mention was made of the assault. I found this rather strange, as well as the fact that no assault charge had been laid against the detective sergeant.

I spoke to the accused's lawyer, and asked why he had not taken any action on the assault.

"Oh, you policemen," he said, "would stick together. My client would look like a fool, trying to defend himself against a charge that he had been injured when he attempted to escape from police custody." Obviously this was the advice he had given to his client.

I told him that he would have been surprised to find that the

RCMP witnesses had no desire to perjure themselves. He found this very hard to believe, and I was sorry to think that this lawyer held the same opinion of the RCMP as he had of the city police, particularly when his client knew that the RCMP had nothing to do with the manner in which he had been injured.

On the basis of the information we had received from the arrested man, we carried out investigations at the plant where he was employed, and also at Hinde and Dauche, where coupons were destroyed for the Oil Controller. At the latter place we found an employee who was also a trafficker, not only of coupons received from our source, but of coupons intended for destruction that he had retrieved from the furnace room. Another line of investigation led us to an ex-employee of the Oil Controller who had been stealing pages of coupons set aside for destruction.

As a result of this one man's information, several members of the black market squad were involved for some weeks investigating and prosecuting approximately twenty-five persons found to be trafficking or in possession of illegal gasoline ration coupons. Those found in possession of coupons illegally were charged with mere possession under the Oil Controller's regulations, and were fined. The traffickers and those who had committed theft were charged with more serious offences under the regulations and the Criminal Code, and punished with the following jail terms:

One - Two years less a day in jail.
One (our informant) - One year in jail.
One - One year.
Three - Six months definite and six months indefinite.
Two - Six months.
One - Three months.
Two - Thirty days.

This was a classic case of how a black market, to be successful, requires a large number of participants. We would have been naive to have thought that even in this case we had found anything but a small proportion of those involved. But we believed we had prosecuted most of the ringleaders.

In 1944, gasoline ration coupons were designed with the intention of making them more difficult to counterfeit. But only a few weeks after the official ration books were distributed, the best counterfeit coupons yet came on the black market. The price for these books of coupons on the black market ranged up to fifty dollars each.

About the same time well-counterfeited food ration coupons appeared. It was obvious to us that the printing and distribution of such coupons was as efficient as that of gasoline coupons. After finding some counterfeit food coupons in the possession of persons arrested for possessing counterfeit gasoline ration coupons, members of the black market squad began checking outlets that used large amounts of butter and sugar in the manufacture of their products.

Rarely did we find one not abusing the rationing regulations. These businesses did not rely on the ration coupon system, but had been granted a quota of rationed goods on the basis of their previous production. Some had abused their quotas. Others had falsified their applications. Still others had used illegal coupons in addition to their quotas. Through the use of the latter, a well-known French pastry shop on Yonge Street obtained tons of butter to which it was not entitled. This resulted in charges being laid. Heavy fines followed. The owner of the patisserie seemed to enjoy the thought of the publicity he would receive, which would show his customers that he was doing everything possible, even breaking the law, to maintain the same quality in his products as he had before food rationing came into effect.

False applications for quotas of rationed goods were not uncommon. One such application had been found by the RCMP in Edmonton. Because the handwriting on the application was not in the handwriting of the woman who had applied for the quota, we were requested to obtain a handwriting sample from her sister in Toronto. They did not say why they suspected this sister of filling in the application. I had taken many handwriting samples in the course of various investigations over the years, but now I did something I had never done before. I asked this woman for a sample of writing not only by her right hand, but also by her left hand as well. Although I could have given no reason for having done so. If a person said he was right-handed, the sample of his right-handed writing was accepted. She objected strongly, saying that she had never written with her left hand.

Normally, I would have expected someone who wrote only with the right hand to have shown me how difficult it was to write with the left hand. I suspected this was a case of "she protesteth too much". So I insisted that she give me a left-handed sample.

Eventually she gave me a left-handed sample. Later I attended the trial in Edmonton in order to give evidence about obtaining it. I was surprised to find that the Toronto woman had been charged along with her sister of conspiring to obtain ration goods illegally. An RCMP handwriting expert from Ottawa proved to the court that the Toronto woman had indeed made out the false applications with her left hand. Both sisters were heavily fined for committing several offences under the food rationing regulations.

I remember this case very clearly, not because of the case itself, but because of what happened during my train journey back to Toronto. In those days travel by air was frowned upon by the RCMP as an unnecessary expense. Later, the RCMP came to realize how much time was wasted by a member sitting on a long train journey, when he could have been at home on the job, and they agreed to air travel.

On this occasion, in wintertime, I was to travel from Edmonton to Winnipeg, changing trains there for Toronto. Weather conditions delayed my train, and by the time it reached Winnipeg, the Toronto train had left for the east. So I changed my ticket for the next train, including one for a sleeping berth. I left Winnipeg that same evening. I woke up about 3 a.m. sensing that the train had been stopped for some time. Lifting the curtain I could see, dimly through the gently falling snow, that we had stopped in deep northern-Ontario woods. I wondered why we had stopped and later learned there was something wrong up ahead.

Eventually the train started and moved very slowly. By now it was daylight, and I was sitting in the dining car having breakfast as we came to a sign marked Sioux Lookout. Through the car windows I could see smashed sleeping cars that had been pulled into a siding. As we passed slowly through this whistle-stop station, I saw several blanket-covered bodies laid out on the platform. A cold chill passed through me. Had I caught the train as intended at Winnipeg, I might have been one of the bodies laid out on the platform or, if I was lucky, one of the many injured passengers who had been rushed to hospital somewhere in northern Ontario.

The wrecked passenger train had been scheduled to pull into a siding to allow another eastbound train the right of way. For some reason it hadn't done so, and the train had ploughed into the back of the passenger train, killing several people in the rear sleeping cars, in one of which I had originally been scheduled to travel.

In the late fall of 1943, a member of the black market squad suspected that permits were being issued by an inspector of the Rubber Controller's office, Eric Sanderson, to persons not entitled to rationed tires. The investigator, when questioning a man suspected of obtaining tires illegally, concluded that a particular tire dealer was able to get permits approved by an inspector although he had little supporting evidence for his application. The signature on the permit was that of Eric Sanderson. On the basis of this information we seized all the tire dealer's records to check on those persons to whom he had sold tires.

As in the case of gasoline rationing, an applicant for new tires filled in an application form, giving all the information required by the Rubber Controller or his representative. He could then form an opinion as to whether a permit could properly be issued for the tires requested. The application required information on such things as proposed mileage, occupation, date of last purchase of tires and so on.

We checked the corresponding records in Sanderson's office. It was clear that the tire dealer, Albert Taube, was getting preferred treatment. Most of Taube's applications seemed to have been completed by two different persons. In each application the occupation and proposed mileage were in the hand of a person other than the one who filled out the body of the application. In those areas the handwriting was that of Eric Sanderson. We sent samples of Sanderson's writing to the RCMP laboratory in Rockcliffe, Ontario, along with the suspected applications for confirmation. The appropriate charges were laid and Sanderson indicated he was going to plead not guilty.

From this point the case was routine, but the number of persons who had to be interviewed required six to eight black market squad members on the investigation, so that it could be completed within a reasonable time.

From these interviews the modus operandi became clear. When a car owner wanted to purchase tires, he went to Taube. Taube knew if he was entitled to tires, but even if not, Taube filled out their applications, except for the two vital questions, occupation and proposed mileage. Taube would then take the applications himself to the Rubber Controller's office, and return with the permits. Our inspection of the applications, and our interviews with the applicants showed that many occupations had been falsified, along with the mileage the applicant proposed to travel.

Sanderson and Taube were charged with conspiring with ten co-conspirators to commit offences against the Wartime Industries Control Board regulations, to wit: the making of false statements in the application for the purchase of rubber tires, and the unlawful issue of false permits. Taube pleaded guilty, but Sanderson pleaded not guilty. Overwhelming evidence was produced by way of forty-five witnesses and 156 documentary exhibits. He was found guilty. Taube, who was called as a Crown witness was fined $500 or three months in jail. Sanderson was sentenced to a three months definite and three months indefinite jail term.

This case showed an inconsistency in the sentencing practices in our courts. I was of the opinion that before another magistrate, Sanderson would have been given at least a year in jail. A number of the persons who had obtained tires illegally through Taube were charged and convicted. All were fined.

Although we believed that Sanderson should have received a more severe punishment, we were pleased that the practice had been stopped. We also believed that he should have been charged under the Criminal Code with breach of trust, but the special prosecutor's view prevailed. This was his first and only prosecution on our behalf. As on so many previous occasions, I wondered how many federal government employees, in positions similar to that of Sanderson, were abusing the trust their employer had placed in them.

This also was one of the many cases where a prosecutor, appointed through patronage, and with no previous experience in prosecuting, failed to appreciate what charges should have been laid against the accused, Sanderson. It might be said that the cause of this was that there were so many black market cases being prosecuted that the federal government was running out of experienced lawyers to be given such patronage appointments.

TWENTY-TWO

Although the war had ended, the rationing of some commodities continued. Price ceilings and other restrictions also remained for some time, so the black market squad was kept busy well into 1947. In the Fall of 1946, the Wartime Prices and Trade Board enforcement counsel in Toronto asked us to investigate a rumour that the wool administrator, a dollar-a-year man, had committed offences under the very regulations he was empowered to enforce. They arose, it was alleged, out of the operation of his own wholesale woollen business.

One of his tasks was to control the amount of woollen cloth allowed to woollen cloth wholesalers. He did this by setting a quota for each wholesaler, based on the amount of business he did before restrictions came into effect. Along with the quota system was a priority system, to ensure that each wholesaler got his supply of woollen goods in turn. Actually, it was a rationing system of the limited amount of woollen cloth that was being milled in Canada, plus what little was being imported from abroad.

Constable Barry Graham undertook the investigation, and he soon learned that the administrator's company had received more wool cloth than his quota allowed. He had abused the priority system by rearranging dates for the delivery of cloth to his company. In this way, it was estimated, the company had received more than $40,000 worth of cloth than that to which it was legally entitled.

As was customary in our investigations, at some appropriate

time during an investigation, an effort was made to obtain a written statement from a suspect. The time had come in this case, and Graham had invited the administrator to the office to obtain his version of the events and, if possible, a signed statement.

Graham kept me advised of his progress, and one very warm day he told me that the wool administrator was coming to the office to be interviewed. When he arrived he was accompanied by his wife. Graham made sure she was comfortably settled in a chair in the main office, while he and her husband went to another office for the interview. From my office I could hear her chatting pleasantly with the other members of the black market squad.

Some time later Graham brought the administrator to my office, and told me that he had taken a written statement, but the administrator would not sign it. He wondered if I could speak to the administrator, to see if I could persuade him to sign the statement in which he had admitted the alleged offences. He sat across from me at my desk while I read the statement. As far as I was concerned, it was a complete confession. Not only did he admit to rearranging the priority dates set out in his own regulations, but also it was clear that he had committed a breach of trust contrary to the Criminal Code.

When I asked what objection he had to signing what he had admitted was a true account of the facts, I expected him to give me reasons for refusing. Instead, much to my surprise, he merely said, "Give me a pen." Without another word he signed the statement, and Graham and I witnessed it.

Meanwhile his wife, who sat in the main office, only a few feet from my open office door, could see and hear what was going on. Because of the heat and the humidity, the only window in the main office was wide open, to catch any breeze coming off Lake Ontario, about half a mile away, in clear view from our second-floor window. Unfortunately for us, a soap factory and a leather tannery stood between our office and the lake, and any breeze wafted unpleasant odours through the window.

Earlier I had gone into the main office to see if our visitor was comfortable.

"Quite comfortable, thank you," she said. She added it was a shame that such a fine group of men as those in the black market squad should work under these unpleasant conditions. "Surely," she continued, "the government could provide better accommodation for their employees than this . . . and so close to those smelly industries!"

I found it unusual that, while her husband was probably confessing to a crime in an adjoining office, she was considering the welfare of men who would be responsible for bringing her husband before the courts on a criminal charge. As the now confessed administrator and his wife were leaving, the latter said to me, "I congratulate you on having such a fine young man as Constable Graham working for you."

Graham laid several charges against the administrator under the wartime regulations, and one for breach of trust under the Criminal Code. The administrator retained two counsel. One was Mr. John J. Robinette, former adviser to the RCMP, and a prosecutor of a few black market cases, now a noted defence counsel. The other was Mr. Eddie Murphy, a heavily built jovial Irishman, who as a former Crown prosecutor had gained a reputation of laughing people into jail. Now a defense counsel, he was reputed to be laughing people out of jail. The Wartime Prices and Trade Board appointed the highly competent Mr. Joseph Singer, Q.C., who had successfully prosecuted many black market cases for us.

Mr. Robinette advised Mr. Singer that the accused wanted to forego a preliminary hearing, and that he wished to go directly for trial before a judge and jury. This was arranged. On the day of the trial we found the judge to be Mr. Justice George Gale, a recent appointee to the Supreme Court of Ontario. Only a month or so earlier he had been appointed a prosecutor for one of our black market cases. He was in the process of preparing it for court when his appointment was announced. This case was to be his first trial as a judge.

By the time of the trial, I had been promoted to the rank of sub/inspector and transferred to Ottawa headquarters. But because I had witnessed the signing of the accused's confession, I had been called as a witness to support the Crown's contention that it had been given quite voluntarily, without any undue pressure from threats or promises.

We knew that when any accused retained the high-priced John J. Robinette as defence counsel, he realized he was in deep trouble, and hoped the clever Mr. Robinette could pull him out of it. We also knew that, in spite of his confession, by going before a judge and jury he had no intention of pleading guilty to the charges. It was also clear that Robinette had been retained in an effort to get the confession thrown out. Nevertheless, it was like old home week for the judge, defence and prosecuting counsel, and members of the RCMP black market squad to meet together, in the same case, in court. We all knew that our previous association would have no effect on how the trial would be conducted, or its outcome.

As the accused stood in the prisoner's box and pleaded not

guilty to the charges read to him, the old adage came to mind. If you are not guilty, be tried by a judge; if guilty by a judge and jury. Graham was the first witness. When it came time for him to describe the taking of the confession, the judge asked the jury to leave the room, and Mr. Robinette requested that I do the same.

I knew that, with us out of the court, the judge would conduct a *voir dire* (a trial within a trial) to establish the voluntariness of the confession. I knew that Robinette knew of the RCMP and their manner of taking statements, but as defence counsel he would accuse Graham of browbeating the accused, or of tricking him into saying what Graham wanted him to say, and promising him leniency if he confessed. Such accusations are all defence counsel's stock in trade. Not only did none of these things take place, but the not unfriendly atmosphere in which the confession was made was an important factor to prove they did not. The fact that the accused's wife was present during most of the proceedings, and her remarks while in our office and when leaving it, would show that nothing untoward had taken place.

Graham knew as well as anyone that if any threat or promise was made, it was enough to have the confession thrown out as evidence. John Robinette knew that if the confession was disallowed, the Crown would have much more difficulty in proving his client guilty. We believed that if this happened we had enough evidence on which the accused could be convicted. The defence might have thought so, too, but eliminating the confession was a matter of first priority.

After Graham, I was called to give evidence in this trial within a trial. Putting on a very serious expression, Robinette's first question to me was, "Did you and Graham discuss the evidence before coming to court?" He was implying that we had got our heads together in order to be able to say the same thing in court.

"Yes, we did," I answered, "during the time we discussed the case with counsel, as we used to do when you prosecuted for us."

I was sure that he had accused Graham of using threats and promises in order to obtain the accused's confession, and I knew the answers Graham had given, because no threats or promises had taken place. This did not prevent Robinette from covering the same ground with me. I could only tell him what had happened in my office when the accused had signed the confession. I pointed out that the accused's wife was sitting in the next office only a few feet away, and that the general atmosphere was not unfriendly.

As I spoke I could see the accused's wife sitting as close to the prisoner's box as she could get, and she knew that what I said was precisely true. I realized that she could give evidence contradicting everything Graham and I had said, but I also knew that if she did she would be committing perjury.

The time came when John Robinette simply repeated questions he had already asked, and when he was about to sit down Mr. Justice Gale asked, "Are you finished, Mr. Robinette?"

Reluctant to release me, Robinette came back toward the witness box.

"Is there anything else you can tell us?" he asked.

It seemed more like a plea than a question, but I knew he was looking for something on which he could base a new round of questioning, to try to show that the confession had been obtained improperly in some way.

"I think so," I answered, knowing how important the atmosphere in which the taking of a confession could be. I described the office set-up. Then I described how the accused's wife sat chatting, how she sympathized with us for having to work in the nauseating odours from the tannery and the soap factory, and how she was sitting only a few feet away from the open door of my office when her husband signed the confession.

From Robinette's demeanor this was hardly what he wanted to hear. It was of no help to him. He sat down.

"If you've no more questions, Mr. Robinette," the judge said, "I'm going to bring the jury back."

Robinette got up immediately. He looked at me for several moments, then asked, "Is there something you can say to help us?" Now he was asking me to provide something on which he could attack Graham's taking of the confession. A strange pleading from a defence counsel to a prosecution witness, and a policeman at that! I thought I had told him everything, but there was one thing I had forgotten until now.

"Yes, I think so, Mr. Robinette," I said.

"Then tell us," he snapped.

"Just as Mrs. —— was leaving the office with her husband, she turned and congratulated me . . . "

This brought a suitable groan from Robinette.

"Now," he said very sarcastically, "why would she want to congratulate you?" He placed great emphasis on the "you".

"For having such a fine young constable as Constable Graham working for me," I answered.

The judge gave a loud laugh, and Robinette sat down again with a groan. He knew he had failed to have the confession thrown out. I was sure that seldom in a court of law had the words of the wife of the accused lauded the good qualities of the policeman who had just taken a confession from her husband. I was equally sure that the judge, who was looking as much for circumstances on which the confession could be disallowed as for reasons why it should be accepted, would be impressed by the circumstances surrounding the taking of the statement, and the unusually friendly attitude of the prisoner's wife toward the police.

Mr. Justice Gale turned to the sheriff sitting on his right.

"Bring in the jury," he said, "and we'll read the statement to them."

Both the prisoner in the box, and his wife in the public seats, knew that everything that Graham and I had said was the exact truth. Later it occurred to me that although one spouse cannot be called upon to give evidence against the other, except in special circumstances, nothing in the law prevents a policeman from quoting, during cross-examination, what one spouse had said to the detriment of the other.

After Robinette's failure to have the confession disallowed, the two defence lawyers seemed to have little interest in the evidence of accountants and others who interpreted the company records, or others who gave pertinent evidence. They called no witnesses on behalf of the accused. The defence lawyers did their best in addressing the jury and asking for a not guilty verdict. But the evidence was overwhelming. The prosecutor's remarks and the charge by the judge were brief. The jury took only about an hour to bring in a guilty verdict.

In sentencing the accused to four years in the penitentiary, the judge stressed the disloyalty of persons who thought only of making money at a time when so many Canadians were risking their lives overseas so that we at home could be safe. Like Mr. Justice Gale, most judges commented scathingly when sentencing persons found guilty of offences under the wartime regulations. But none were more scathing than Judge Ian McDonnell of the York County Court, during a case in which he was sentencing a man found guilty of trafficking in counterfeit gasoline ration coupons.

I have no sympathy with the accused," he said "Hundreds of young Canadians are willing to give their lives, and in many cases have given their lives, for our cause. Many have given up prominent careers at tremendous personal cost. The contribution of the accused is to sabotage wartime regulations. In another country the penalty would probably be death.

Defence counsel in this case pleaded for a light sentence, because his client had already been disgraced.

"He should be disgraced," Judge McDonnell said.

The wool administrator's case, like similar cases we had prosecuted involving breach of trust on the part of a government official, made me wonder, as I did in each similar case, how many other employees, administering wartime regulations throughout Canada, had taken advantage of their own positions to abuse the regulations for monetary gain.

During the four years that the very active Toronto black market squad dealt with a relatively minor part of the black market that existed in Canada, we were continuously amazed at the disregard so many Canadians, in all walks of life, had for the regulations aimed at ensuring the fair distribution of consumer goods. It was a sad commentary on the manner in which a large number of Canadians failed to accept relatively minor responsibilities in time of war.

Mention of Mr. Justice Gale, in the above case, reminds me of the special prosecutors who handled our black market cases and became judges in the Ontario Supreme Court. Some became Chief Justices. They included Mr. Justice J.C. McRuer, Mr. Justice John Wilson and Mr. Justice J.D. Arnup. Mr. Dalton Wells, Enforcement counsel of the Wartime Prices and Trade Board in Toronto, was also appointed to the Supreme Court and later became a Chief Justice. Mr. John J. Robinette, long after he worked for us, was appointed a judge in the Supreme Court, but resigned within a few days. Two of our most able prosecutors, Mr. Norman L. Mathews and Mr. Joseph Singer, did not receive such appointments, for reasons of which I am not aware.

Not all the lawyers appointed to prosecute for us, however, were of such high caliber as those who became judges. Several times I reported on the ineptness of lawyers appointed as prosecutors, and asked that they not be appointed again. One lawyer, for example, never made any decision in court without saying to the magistrate, "I will have to ask the RCMP about that." But as the appointees names were taken from the Liberal government's patronage list, they were frequently re-appointed. There was never any doubt in my mind that all the appointments, even of the above-mentioned lawyers to judgeships, resulted from their adherence to the Liberal Party, although that did not necessarily detract from their abilities. Not one known Conservative Party adherent was appointed as a special prosecutor in our cases, and I believe the same policy applied to RCMP cases in other parts of Canada. Politics is politics, even in wartime.

APPENDIX I

Undercover RCMP Work

Some undercover police work has been described in this book. It is often the only method that can succeed in certain crimes. Undercover work may be for either short or long periods of time. A short period, for example, occurs when a suspect has been arrested and a disguised policeman is placed in a cell next to his in order to find out more about the crime or crimes that he has committed.

Long periods of undercover work are usually required in drug cases in which a number of policemen are involved. In such cases undercover policemen, or civilians being employed by the police for such work, may find it impossible to avoid committing offences themselves in order to further the investigation. This is acceptable where the police investigate for the purpose of bringing criminal activity to an end and the criminals to justice.

Police do not decide to conduct undercover work unless the crime involved is important enough for such a method, and normal police procedures will be ineffective. This is often the case in drug investigations. Undercover work is not necessarily done by a solitary policeman. It sometimes involves many undercover policemen, as well as other policemen, to supervise and direct the investigation. Even a single policeman who is in undercover work requires close supervision.

The undercover operator, whether policeman or civilian, must deceive those persons with whom he associates, and from whom he wishes to obtain information about a crime already committed or being planned. This deceit evokes much criticism when such a matter reaches court. It comes mostly from defence counsel, whose main responsibility is to get his client free of the charge. Occasionally, criticism of undercover work may come from judges who have a repugnance for the method, in spite of the jurisprudence built up over centuries to support it.

Considering the circumstances under which undercover work is conducted, it is easy to see how the undercover person can be accused of encouraging the commission of a crime. However, the police invariably know that a crime has been committed or planned before they decide to use such a police method.

At a trial involving undercover evidence, it is usual for defence counsel to try to persuade the court that if the offence had not been instigated by the undercover agent, his "innocent client" would not have been "trapped" by the police. It is true that an accused person in such cases does get trapped by having an undercover agent present when he is doing or saying things that will be used against him at his trial. But jurisprudence supports the agent, if in the course of an investigation he makes false representations, and even takes part in committing the crime, as long as the prosecution is able to show that he has not instigated the crime. The undercover agent is present in order to collect evidence which can be used to prosecute the criminal. This may take the form of describing how the crime was committed, or what conversations took place between the police agent and an accused person about a crime already committed, or even about crimes he intends to commit. The motives of the two are completely different. For that reason, and because the undercover policeman is not an accomplice, his evidence need not be corroborated.

When choosing a policeman for undercover work, appearance is a serous consideration. He must act as if he is familiar with his surroundings. If he is to work in a business milieu he must act as a businessman. If he is investigating a drug case, often he will fit in best if he looks anemic and is poorly clothed.

One judge who found police undercover work repugnant was Mr. Justice Stuart of the Alberta Appeal Court, even though jurisprudence built up over centuries supported it. Nevertheless he remarked:

> As long as the law permits the employment by the Crown of so-called "stool-pigeons", I do not think we should allow any repugnance to that system to influence

our decision with regard to the intention of the Legislature in the use of the words in question. Indeed the fact that, after several expressions of repugnance by individual members of the court, of which I have been one, the Legislatures have not interfered, seems to me to be fairly good proof that in the public interest if it is advisable, or at least considered by the Legislatures to be advisable, not to forbid the practice.

Unlike Mr. Justice Stuart, who reluctantly accepted the evidence of an undercover agent as the law intended, Judge Parker, of the York County Court in Ontario, dismissed an appeal from a magistrate's conviction on charges under wartime regulations. He commented:

The evidence on which I am asked to convict is the the evidence of a man who goes out and confesses he deliberately lies to produce the offence, therefore, it is reasonable to expect, and I must give consideration to that phase, a man who would go out and lie to obtain an offence and induce an offence, how far will he go to stretching the truth to obtain a conviction . . . ?

The undercover policeman, in this case, had posed as an ordinary civilian. He did not identify himself as a policeman when he went to purchase a used car above the ceiling price, contrary to wartime motor vehicle regulations. The Crown appealed Judge Parker's decision to the Supreme Court of Ontario, as provided in wartime regulations. (R. V. White No.2 84 ccc, p.144). Mr. Justice Laidlaw, one of the appeal judges, all of whom concurred with his views, had this to say about the constable's behaviour:

With much respect, I am of the opinion that the learned judge improperly discredited the police constable. I can see no reason to criticize his conduct in any way, but on the contrary, am impressed with the view that he was carrying out his duty as a peace officer of the law in a proper and necessary manner under the circumstances. That he resorted to false representations or disguise for the purpose of obtaining the evidence does not necessarily discredit him or invalidate his evidence.

Mr. Justice Gillanders, an associate justice of the court, commented on another aspect of undercover police work:

. . . and as something has been said during the argument about the employment of "stool-pigeons", so-called, this is an opportune time to make some observations thereon in the public interest, because the law and the practice in that behalf continue to be persistently and harmfully misrepresented in various quarters which misrepresentations have tended to hamper and impede police officers, magistrates and others in the discharge of their duties to see that the law is enforced according to long-established legal precedent and usage . . .

The court directed that the case be returned to the County court for its views to be taken into account. This was done and the accused pleaded guilty before Judge Parker. Although the judge imposed a relatively small fine, the important fact was that the police undercover method of investigating crime had been strongly supported by one of the highest courts in the country.

It is clear from the above that when an undercover policeman lends himself to a scheme for the purpose of curtailing crime, it seems quite unfair to stigmatize him when he is doing no more than his proper legal duty, supported as he is by at least a century of jurisprudence.

APPENDIX II

The Rule of Silence

During my police career I have encountered court rules that hinder the police in the gathering of evidence, and prevent courts from convicting the guilty. These rules began to develop more than three hundred years ago, in an attempt to counteract the outrageously unfair trial system of that time.

In those days courts forced confessions from accused persons, sometimes through torture. Hearsay was admitted. Juries consisted of the judge and crown witnesses. Witnesses could not be cross-examined, and the accused could not call witnesses on his own behalf. At one time accused persons could not have counsel to act on their behalf. When at last they were allowed counsel, counsel was not allowed to cross-examine witnesses, and could only address the court on points of law. The accused were not allowed to give evidence because they were not allowed to be sworn. This gave counsel grounds for pleading with juries, such as they were, that their accused clients could not defend themselves because they could not give evidence.

After 1640 witnesses were allowed to give evidence, but were still not permitted to be sworn, in case their evidence damaged the credibility of crown witnesses. A witness, not being sworn, was thought to be lying if his evidence contradicted that of a prosecution witness. Evidence of the accused's bad character was freely given.

Evidence in written form was accepted by the court without the writer appearing, and the evidence of an accomplice, obtained under torture,was accepted as though freely given.

Slowly, over the centuries, very necessary changes were made in the rules of evidence, and new ones established to ensure that accused persons received a fair trial. Today an accused person is presumed innocent until proven guilty, and his guilt must be beyond a reasonable doubt. One rule allows the accused to remain silent, the rule of silence or self-incrimination. Under this rule, an accused is not required to assist the court in obtaining as much truth as possible, concerning the matter before it, from the person most likely to be the most knowledgeable about it. And in remaining silent the accused helps to create some of the doubt which may ultimately benefit him.

Jeremy Bentham, a noted English reformer, usually a champion of the underdog, in 1830 had the following to say about the rule of silence:

> This rule is one of the most pernicious and irrational rules that ever found its way into the human mind. If criminals of every class had assembled and framed a system after their own wishes, is this not the rule the very first they would have established for their own security? Innocence never takes advantage of it; innocence claims the right of speaking, as guilt invokes the privilege of silence.

This rule has been carried over into police interrogations. When a person is suspected of having committed a crime the police are required to warn him in the following or similar words:

> You need not say anything. You have nothing to hope from any promise or favour, and nothing to fear from any threat whether or not you say anything. Anything you do say may be used as evidence at your trial.

It is the rule of silence, coupled with the police warning, that forms the basis of a counsel's advice to his client when he tells him to "keep your mouth shut" when the police wish to question him. Counsel cannot be blamed for this attitude when the rule of silence invites it.

Glanville Williams, a British critic of court rules, when commenting on the rules of silence, put it another way.

Historically regarded, the rule against questioning the defendant (in court) is one example of the indifference of society to the need for securing the conviction of the guilty.

In 1964 the British government asked its Criminal Law Revision Committee to consider balancing the security of the community and its law-abiding citizens against the rights of an accused. The government specifically asked the committee what could be done to modify the rules that had ceased to be appropriate to modern conditions.

Regarding the accused's right to silence, the committee recommended that after a *prima facie* case has been made out against an accused at his trial, he should be invited in open court to give, under oath, his story, on which he could be cross-examined. He would not be forced to do so, nor punished for not doing so. But any refusal could be taken into account when the judge considered his guilt or innocence. As a result the British courts now follow the committee's recommendation.

As far back as 1931, the American National Commission of Law Observance commented on this same rule. In commenting that a trial was more of a game than a sincere effort to get at the truth, one report stated that the privilege to remain silent "has come to be of little advantage to the innocent and a mere piece in the game of criminal justice."

This is only one of the many comments made in various writings about the criminal trial being a "sport".

No doubt all judges are aware of the difficulties, created by the rule of silence, in obtaining as much truth as possible about matters before them in a criminal trial. But it appears that only one judge has publicly spoken out about it. In 1970, Mr. Justice Edson Haines of the Ontario Supreme Court, in a rare public speech, included the following:

> I submit that the greatest obstacle to efficient criminal law enforcement in the Anglo-American jurisdiction is the right of the accused to remain silent. It is a luxury society can no longer afford. It contributes to the high success ratio of crime. It frustrates the police, comforts the criminals, and encourages disrespect for the law. And in great deference to the legal profession, the abolition of the right to remain silent is necessary to save an honourable profession from its own dishonour.

If Mr. Justice Haines thought that publicizing his views would bring any change, he was mistaken. If Canadian legal authorities discussed his views on possible changes in the rule of silence, no word reached the Canadian public.

This same judge believed so strongly in the need for changes in the criminal trial system that, in the same speech, he voiced his opinion on other changes he would like to see, and his reasons for doing so:

> If our Canadian courts used the same rules to try civil cases that are used to try criminal cases, the Canadian public would soon find a better way of resolving its disputes. The civil and economic life of the Anglo-American world is dependent for resolution of disputes upon a system of the complete ability of all parties to testify. Why should an accused in a criminal case have such advantages requiring full disclosure of the case for the prosecution while making no disclosure of his own, and the right to avoid questioning during preliminary hearing proceedings and at the trial by simply staying out of the witness box? Is it not about time the accused was made equally compellable to disclose what has occurred? Can society demand any less where it has made out a case to be answered?

Many Canadian will agree with Mr. Justice Haines. But if, as it seems, it is impossible to have the rule of silence modified, there is little likelihood that his other suggestions will ever come under scrutiny. It is to be wondered why the relatively mild change made in the rule of silence by the British cannot be put into effect in Canadian criminal trials.

Although the police are often criticized for the state of crime, and the courts criticized for their leniency in dealing with criminals, both are hampered by the rule of silence. There is no lack of suggestions of how the courts and the police can improve their efficiency. But never is it heard in the right places that perhaps a modification in the rule of silence would go far to ensure greater efficiency on the part of the courts and the police. Any change that would allow greater access to the truth would result in more efficient policing, and make it less likely that criminal trials will be referred to as a "sport".

APPENDIX III

The Philosophy of the Royal Canadian Mounted Police

by D/Commr. W.H. Kelly (retired)
(Reproduced from the RCMP *Quarterly*, Spring 1997)

The following article was written by D/Commr. Kelly (retired) at the request of Commissioner Nicholson in 1956, and appeared in the 1956/1958 Canada Year Book. This article is just as pertinent today because it shows us that as much as things change, we need to continually focus on our raison d'etre, our values (philosophy), on quality service, and on our communities. It demonstrates to us how little things have changed, and that if we wish to remain the police service of choice, we must focus on the ideals that gave us the public support that we currently enjoy. D/Commr. Kelly's article also reinforces the Shared Leadership Vision process, and how the values that our employees feel are important have changed very little. – Ed.

If the philosophy of the Royal Canadian Mounted Police had to be expressed in one work, that word would be "service".

Service to the individual and to the community has always been the theme of the Force. It began when the North-West Mounted Police went to the prairies in 1873-74, at which time it was essentially a frontier and a rural police force. The opportunity to give greater service arose in 1920 when, as the Royal Canadian Mounted Police, the organization acquired new responsibilities as its field of operation included the whole of Canada. Since that time still greater opportunities have arisen as the Force has accepted certain provincial as well as wider federal duties.

The service given by the Force has included dealing with problems encountered by pioneers in Western Canada and the North, combatting Canada's illicit drug traffic, preventing smuggling on the coasts and the United States border, policing rural areas from coast to coast, patrolling the Arctic and providing Canada's security service. In performing these duties a strong sense of service has developed in individual members, and this represents the real strength of the Force.

In order to handle its original responsibilities and to survive the conditions under which it was to function, the Force was organized as a semi-military body. Because this kind of organization has proved of lasting value, it has continued as such to the present day. The training of present-day recruits and the work of the Force are, therefore, carried out in a semi-military atmosphere.

It is not correct, however, to say that Royal Canadian Mounted Police discipline is military discipline. Rather it is a discipline that serves the unique needs of the Force, which recognizes that discipline must be intelligently enforced in an organization of some 4,500 members [17,500 in 1997-98] spread over the whole of Canada. During training the recruit is impressed with the need for a willingness to accept discipline, in order for the organization to provide the public with service of a high quality.

The Royal Canadian Mounted Police officer is impressed with the idea that public esteem for the law and its administration depends in large part on the behaviour of the police officer who enforces that law. It is of vital importance that the police officer's behaviour be exemplary.

The Force insists that discipline, as it pertains to its members, must set moral standards, and that standards accepted by the average citizen may not be high enough for a police officer. Thus members must at all times act in accord not only with the letter of the law, but also with the spirit of the law, including moral law. Unless they are prepared to adopt this as their own attitude, they cannot approach their duties in the manner required of them.

In addition to the need for discipline, the Force stresses the need for a strong sense of public service, initiative, independence of mind, and a readiness to adapt to changing conditions. These qualities are essential to the success of every member of the Royal Canadian Mounted Police, and training is aimed at giving everyone the opportunity of acquiring them.

An effort is made to show all members, as early as possible, why these traits are desirable, not only for the sake of the Royal Canadian Mounted Police but also for the country as a whole. At the same time, however, the Force realizes that it is not possible to convey the full meaning of public service until members have had experience and have developed a satisfaction from their work.

The word "service" means different things to different people. To members of the Royal Canadian Mounted Police, as distinct from most other public servants, it must be related to what the public, in a democracy such as is found in Canada, requires of its police forces. All members of the Royal Canadian Mounted Police, from their earliest days in training, have been impressed with the fact that in spite of their powers as peace officers, which are given them to carry out their many duties, their rights are no more than those of any other citizen. They are also impressed with the fact that although it is their duty to investigate crime, it is the courts of the country which assess the evidence collected against individuals, and which decide whether such evidence warrants a conviction and subsequent punishment. All members of the Force must realize that their work, though important, is only a segment of the administration of the law, and that they themselves must be scrupulously careful always to act within that law.

The Royal Canadian Mounted Police has proved that, given a sound sense of service, it is not difficult to set high standards of service. However, the Force considers it is not sufficient simply to appeal to idealism. Conditions of service receive attention at all levels, so that members can develop a pride in their leaders and in their organization. Also, efforts are made to see that members develop a sense of accomplishment, both in themselves as individuals and in the Force as a whole.

A sense of individual accomplishment is developed not only through a member's work, but also through his or her superiors paying attention to personal progress and development, and through each member being allowed to gain recognition and promotion for initiative, industriousness and devotion to duty.

The sense of accomplishment on a Force-wide basis is developed through a knowledge of the history of the Force, its present responsibilities, and its place in the development of Canada. The

Force endeavours, too, to carry forward from the past all traditions of proven value, a task probably made easier by the fact that its past is both colourful and inspiring, and that the organization is still of vital importance to Canada.

Ever since its inception as the North-West Mounted Police, the first aim of the Force, as of all police forces in democratic countries, has been the prevention of crime. The detection of crime has always come second in importance.

Both prevention and detection today, however, demand vastly different methods of procedure from those of early days. Modern methods of living and modern methods of commerce and industry enable criminals to commit crimes with methods not formerly possible. Crimes arising out of business are more prevalent than ever. Crimes arising out of the use of automobiles are on the increase. Speed enables criminals to leave scenes of crimes quickly, only to commit similar crimes at distant points. The police of today know they can combat modern criminals only by using modern police methods.

The realization of the need for modern methods has had a great influence on the Royal Canadian Mounted Police. Scientific laboratories have been set up, staffed by laboratory detectives who are more than a match for the criminals they contend with. Young police officers are trained to understand and recognize modern and scientific criminal methods. They are also trained to understand and to use or to avail themselves of scientific methods for combatting crime, whether the crime is committed by scientific methods or not. Police officers in the field, on whom the scientific laboratories depend, are given extensive courses in scientific crime detection, both in their initial training and from time to time throughout their careers. This leads to a constant awareness of modern and scientific methods during daily work, at all levels of the organization.

A further aspect of Royal Canadian Mounted Police development lies in its growing links with other police forces. The value to the public of co-operation between the Royal Canadian Mounted Police and other police forces in Canada and in other parts of the world, through the International Criminal Police Organization and similar bodies, becomes more evident each day. Indeed, in its unique position as a police force with federal, provincial and municipal responsibilities, the Royal Canadian Mounted Police is increasingly aware of the need for the closest co-operation, not only among police forces, but with all agencies engaged in combatting crime.

The Royal Canadian Mounted Police realize that the attitude of the public toward the police force depends in large part on the police officer the public meets personally, whether on a prairie farm, on the highway, or on the beat in a large city. The Force realizes further, that a police force may be up-to-date in every respect, but unless relations between the police and the public lead citizens to identify themselves with their police force, a desirable situation will not exist. They believe it is this sense of citizen-police identification which develops public confidence in the police. They know that without this confidence, which is a basic ingredient for the success of any police force in a democracy, police work becomes difficult if not impossible.

Members of the Force, therefore, are encouraged to approach their work with a sincere desire to develop good public relations. Indeed, the aim is to provide well-trained, courteous police officers who will win the confidence of the public by serving with efficiency and zeal, and who will, also, merge with and be a respected part of the community in which they live.

Although the Royal Canadian Mounted Police believes itself fortunate in being classed as a corps which has given, and is now giving, good service to the Canadian public, it feels no complacency in this regard.

On the contrary, it believes that present performance should be used mainly as a measure for raising standards in the future. With this in mind, its purpose is to develop in its members an ever increasing sense of loyalty and pride in the Force. In this way, it is endeavouring to improve the quality of service which it hopes is now synonymous in the minds of Canadian citizens with the name "Royal Canadian Mounted Police".

The author, now 88, joined the Force 66 years ago, in 1933. D/commr. Kelly served on detachment in "F" Division, Saskatchewan, and in the Criminal Investigation Branch (CIB) in "O" Division, Ontario. He was commissioned in 1946 and subsequently served as the Personnel Officer in nine divisions. In 1951, he was posted overseas, where he worked as Liaison Officer with European police and security organizations, then as the OIC, Visa Control, until 1954. Upon his return to Canada, Kelly worked as the Chief Preventive Officer at Headquarters and in 1959, he was promoted to Assistant Director, Security and Intelligence (S&I); five years later, in 1964, he was made Director, S&I. In 1967, Kelly was promoted to Deputy Commissioner Operations, and after 37 years of dedicated service with the RCMP, he retired in 1970. Since then, D/Commr. Kelly has written several books related to the Force, with Mrs. Kelly, an author in her own right, as co-author or editor. He has also published many articles in the Quarterly. – Ed.

Other RCMP-Related Books
Published by Centax Books/Publishing Solutions/PW Group

Red Coats on the Prairies –
The North-West Mounted Police 1886-1900
by William Beahen and Stan Horrall
Here is the real story, the incredible adventures, the daunting hardships, the personal and political scandals, the rigorous training, the frontier morals and mores. Using original source material and documents, RCMP historians Beahen and Horrall cut through the romantic fantasies to expose the real heroes. They document the influential role of the NWMP on the political, social and cultural life of the developing western community. An accurate account and a compelling read, Red Coats, shows how the image of the mounties took shape on the prairies.

Retail $59.95   Hard Cover   8½" x 11"
400 pages   61 period photographs
English-ISBN 1-894022-01-7   French-ISBN 1-894022-02-5

Sam Steele: Lion of the Frontier
Robert Stewart
An official book of the March West. Sam Steele was a policing legend during legendary times. This lively and vital history is the definitive story of an intrepid individual living in extraordinary times. One of the first members of the North-West Mounted Police, he trained men and established posts in a land that was alive with danger. Sam Steele's bravery, endurance and sense of fair play became a legend of the frontier. A champion of the Indians, he earned their confidence and respect. His men went after cattle rustlers, horse thieves and murderers, controlled border traffic and policed the construction of the CPR. During the Gold Rush he dealt with wanton lawlessness under the most extreme conditions. Absorbing, exciting and true, here is a first-rate epic about a policing pioneer during a critical time in Canada's history.
Retail $59.95   Hard Cover   8½" x 11"
320 pages   200 historic photographs and maps
ISBN 1-894022-23-8

These books are available at book stores, or for ordering information, contact Centax Books and Distribution at:
• Phone: 1-800-667-5595 • Fax: 1-800-823-6829
• Email: centax@printwest.com